A HISTORY OF
UPTON AND
BERRYWOOD

Fred Golby – Local Historian

Fred Golby's early life began in Alma Street, St James. His education began and ended in St. James Church of England School, which he left when he was fourteen.

He started work on his father's Nursery in Duston Mill Lane. Then in 1947 the land was acquired in Mill Way for a second nursery.

Today, after 73 years of this family business, the Millway Nursery is now a Garden Centre, though most of the original land has now been taken away for roads etc.

Some 25 years ago his interest in local history began, with his accumulation of old photographs. For many years these were used for showing the fascinating industrial and village life of what is now part of West Northampton.

The quarterings once found at Upton on the coats of arms belonging to Upton Hall.

Cover photographs:

St. Michael's Church, Upton

Berrywood Tower

Upton Hall

2

Acknowledgements: Berrywood

Northamptonshire Health Authority for being given access to Berrywood Hospital old annual accounts. My thanks to the many retired nurses and officials (male and female): Mr. Beadle, (late) Mr. A. Clements, Mr. R. Kempster, Mr. W. Burrell, Mrs. R. Billingham, Miss G. Billingham, Mrs M. Davis, Mrs. Scott, Mrs. E. Munday, Mrs. M. Gough, Mrs. R. Rowell, Mr. J. Thompson, Mr. W. Bailey (Canada), John Smeathers.

Acknowledgements: Upton

Quinton House School, Walter Spokes, John Spokes, Miles Still, David Still, Mr. Rob Webb,

Mrs. Ryan, Mrs. Norris, Dr. Sargant, The Venerable Basil Marsh,

Mr. R. Tricker (Churches Conservation Fund Historian).

Royal Ordnance Survey

Northamptonshire Record Office

Northamptonshire Libraries

Northampton Mercury Ltd.

John Smeathers for final reading

Mary Smeathers for researching Berrywood photos

Office staff – Wendy Sharland, Rita Redley, and Leanne Sharland.

My sincere apologies to anyone who has helped me with this book if I have failed to acknowledge them.

Published by J. W. F. Golby

Copyright 1994

ISBN 0 9518569 2 8

Printed and bound in Great Britain by
Warwick Printing Company Limited, Theatre Street, Warwick CV34 4DR.
London Office: Granville House, 112 Bermondsey Street, London SE1 3TX.

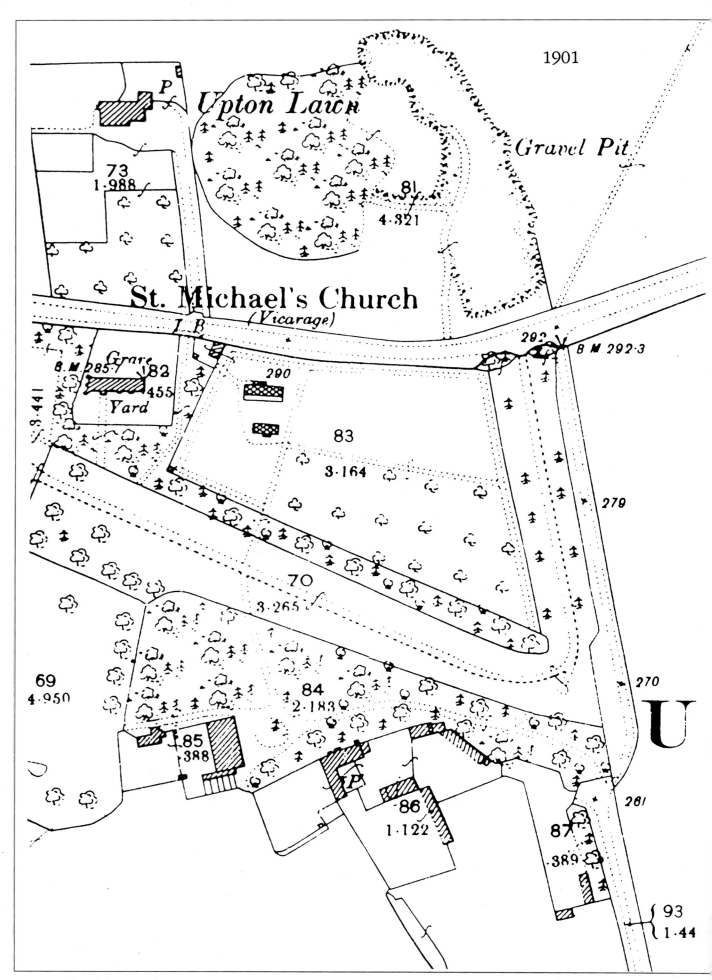

St. Michael's Church
(Vicarage)

Introduction to Upton

Upton parish land of almost a 1,000 acres will soon be part of the expanding Northampton, with its easy access to the M1 and the rail link. This is a history of the old village which included Berrywood originally a farm on the estate. The Hall dates back from Monastic times.

In the 250 years of the Samwells' history at Upton, the family showed their loyalty to the crown as royal sequestrators, firstly helping capture the conspirators in this county in the Gunpowder plot and later holding the same authority during the restoration of Charles II.

Today the church of St. Michaels is in the hands of the Churches Conservation Trust who keep the fabric of the church in good order. When the building was closed in 1980 for worship a group of people formed the Friends of Upton Church, under the then Archdeacon, the Venerable Basil Marsh, to care for the interior, and have an annual Dedication and Harvest Festival service, which occurs, at the end of September. It was realised at the end of 1980 that this west side of Northampton would sooner or later be developed for housing. So all the valuable artifacts of St. Michael's organ, font, brass lantern, have been taken to other churches, and used until such times as they are again needed, and returned. Quinton House School who occupy the Hall now use the Church for occasional services for the pupils, and have given wonderful help in keeping the church clean and presentable for visitors.

150 years ago the entire acreage of the estate consisted of four farms. Now the Spokes families continue to farm most of the land from Duston Mill and Lodge Farm.

F. Golby

Part One – Upton Hall

In mediaeval times there was a village at Upton. At the death of Richard Knightley in 1477 there were 24 houses standing but in 1700 only 11 houses, and only four in the census of 1801. Going down Upton Mill Rd on the right hand side one can see the outline of the old village in the uneven grass areas. Years ago the old gardeners told me to look for the lines of clumps of nettles that used to grow where stone foundations were near the surface. This gave you a clear outline of the properties in this field all those years ago. The presence of the foundations meant that the ground had never been turned by the plough. The remains of the old time saw pits and remains of the auxiliary buildings adjacent to the road are still visible. Many villages near large ancestral homes were demolished. Some argue that the gentry did not want workers living in cottages near them. Others say it was the great change to all grazing and sheep which required a minimum of labour.

One must look to the west part of the hall to see the age of the old house. Its early sandstone probably came from Duston pits not far away. The Victorians have replaced the old windows and doors. It is there we find the deep cellars and high old loft rooms steeped in age and legend. Again in Regency times the whole of the west front was rebuilt in brick and a dummy second story was added, a brick wall built in the eaves of this old roof with windows with blank shutters behind, which does give the whole frontage dignity and character.

Here is a writer's history of the owners of the Manor of Upton published in 1849 –

"Manor – The King himself held Optone which consisted of two hides of land, at the time of the Doomsday-survey. There was a mill of the yearly rent of 12s. 8d. and 6 acres of meadow, and half a hide at Harleston pertained to this manor, the whole of which was valued, as in the time of Kind Edward, at £15 yearly. The manor of Upton continued in the hands of the Crown till the reign of Henry II, when it was given with its appurtenances to Robert Fitz-Sewin, otherwise called Robert de Chaunceux, of Northampton. By inquisition taken in the reign of Henry III, John de Chaunceux was certified to hold the manor of Upton, with the hundred of Newbottle-Grove belonging to it, by the serjeanty of finding one armed soldier in the King's army in time of war for 40 days at his own cost. The manor thus continued in the possession of this family till the 21st of Edward III. (1348), when Nicholas de Chaunceux died seized of it, and was succeeded by Nicholas Paries. By inquisition taken at his death, he was found to hold this manor of the king in (capite), by the service of finding an armed soldier for 40 days within the four seas at his own expense, and a bailiff to execute the sheriff's writs within the hundred of Newbottle-Grove. Roesia, the wife of Nicholas Paries died seized of this lordship in the 31st of this reign (1358), and was succeeded by Richard, the son of William de Clendon, who obtained the King's licence in the 21st of Richard II. (1398), to enfeoff Nicholas de Hilton and William de Grendon, in the said lordship and hundred. He afterwards conveyed them William Grendon, John Kydlington, and Walter Clendon, who in the 7th Henry V. (1420), were fined 10 marks for the offence of purchasing the premise without licence from the Crown. The same year they were sold by them to Richard Knightley, Esq., in which family they continued till about the year 1600, when Sir Richard Knightley sold them to William Samwell, Esq., of Northampton" (afterwards knighted)., for £7,366. (Wellan).

Baker's history of the early 19th Century records all the Samwell portraits, then in the Hall and elsewhere in the house many full length portraits are attributed to famous Dutch and English painters and contained a collection of portraits relative to the family.

The Hall or Saloon, which is lofty and spacious, contained nine large full length portraits of Richard Samwell; Richard Samwell, esq. his eldest son; Sir Thomas Samwell, 1st bart.; Sir Thomas Samwell, 2nd bart. with his son Thomas, afterwards 3rd bart., and three of his daughters; the three daughters and coheiress of Thomas 2nd Viscount Wenman Frances, wife of Richard Samwell, esq. *Lely;* Penelope, 2nd wife of Sir Thomas Cave, of Stanford, 1st baronet, *Lely;* and Elizabeth, wife of Greville Verney, of Compton Murdak in Warwickshire, esq. *Lely;* Thomas, 2nd Viscount Wenham, habited in black, and seated in a chair; and Charles, King of Sweden. In this apartment also are portraits of Mary, daughter and coheiress of Thomas Catesby, by Margaret Samwell, and wife of Henry (Paget) 1st Earl of Uxbridge; Dame Milicent, 1st wife of Sir Thomas Samwell, 2nd bart; and Dame Mary, his 2nd wife; Sir William Fermor, ancestor of the Earl of Pomfret, *Vandyck;* Sir John Finet, master of the ceremonies to King James 1st.

Quinton House have produced a pamphlet available at the school describing the pictures that today remain in the large Saloon.

The old monastic buildings with the small windows in the old monk's room. (Who sought seclusion there?)

Old drawing of Samwell's Tomb and Coat of arms in All Saints prior to the great fire of Northampton.

SAMWELL MONUMENT IN ALL SAINTS' CHURCH, NORTHAMPTON.

Rothersthorpe Church Pulpit 1579 with the initials of Francis Samwell who owned that estate at that time.

Old medieval part of the Hall showing bell to call the squire if on the estate.

The memorial to Jane Harrington in Milton Church.

West view of Dower House, Duston. The older part of the House was built by Thomas Samwell Watson Samwell in 1822.

The Georgian windows in the Dower House, same design as Upton Hall.

The old Manor House at Milton Malsor, in the 16th Century home of James Harrington who married Jane, daughter of Sir William Samwell.

One of the West Georgian Windows at Upton Hall showing the Squirrels coat of arms of the Samwells.

The stone slab in Gayton Church commemorating the death of Jane Harrington in 1662.

From a Print in the British Museum, engraved by M. Van der Gucht
after a painting by Sir Peter Lely.

James Harrington with family coat of arms.

Cottesford Manor, Oxfordshire, home of the Samwells in the early 16th Century.

Gayton Manor which was purchased in the 16th Century by Sir William Samwell.

Samwell's coat of arms in the beautiful plaster work in the Saloon of Upton Hall.

15th Century wall plaque in Cottesford Church to Richard Samwell's family.

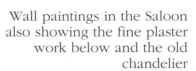

Wall paintings in the Saloon also showing the fine plaster work below and the old chandelier

(Photo taken from the Minstrel Gallery)

The 19th Century also contained in the Pink Drawing Room. Lucy Countess of Bedford, sister and countess of John 2nd Lord Harrington, Honthorstl Rev. Thomas Fuller, d.d rector of Hatfield in Hertfordshire, *Kneller;* Milicent, his 2nd wife, daughter of Adrian Munday, esq. and widow of John Musters, esq of Colwick in Nottinghamshire, Kneller; a fortune-telling pieces, supposed to be portraits, *Mercier;* and Sir Richard Samwell. Study. Old portraits on board, probably copies from Holbein, of Edward 4th; Edward 6th; Mary; Philip King of Spain, her husband; and James I; Oliver Cromwell, *Olivar;* Buffardin, musician to the King Poland. Gothic Room. Sir Adolphus Oughton, bart. *Mercier;* Sir Thomas Samwell, 2nd bart. *Mercier;* Sir Thomas Samwell, 3rd bart. *Mercier;* Christopher Saul, esq. Sir Clement Edmondes, of Preston Deanry, member of the city of London, and a clerk of the privy council to James I, a fine head by an unknown artist; George 2nd Earl of Halifax in his robes; John Bales, of Northampton, ob. A.D. 1705, aged 127 years. Dining Room. Over the chimney is a large and interesting bacchanalian group, by *Mercier,* representing Sir Thomas Samwell, the 2nd baronet, attended by his favourite black servant Caesar Parisetti, seated at a table drinking Burgundy with his friends John Neale, of Allesley in Warwickshire, esq.; General de Jean; and John Floyd, esq. who, as president, is crowned with a chaplet of vine leaves. In this room are two fine portraits of an unknown lady and gentleman, and a few cabinet pictures. Staircase, etc. Godfrey Clarke, of Chilcot in Derbyshire, esq.; Lady Catherine his wife, daughter of Philip 2nd Earl of Chesterfield; Elizabeth Samwell, 1st wife of Sir John Langham, of Cottesbrook, 4th bart.; Sir William Samwell; Sir Thomas Parkyns, of Bunny in Nottinghamshire, 1st bart. *Lely;* Charles I and Henrietta his queen, Vandyck; Sir William Humble, of Thorp Underwood, 5th bart; Dame Elizabeth his wife, sister of Henry 1st Earl of Darlington; Thomas Catesby, of Whiston and Ecton, esq. *Lely;* Margaret Samwell, his wife, *Lely;* James Harrington, esq. author of Oceana; and the following by *Mercier* – Sir Thomas Samwell, 2nd bart; Sir Arthur Hesilrige, of Northampton, 7th bart.; Robert Andrew, of Harleston, esq. the last of the first line; John Neale, of Allesley in Warwickshire, esq.; General de Jean, of the 3rd Caribineers; and John Lord Ligonier, of Ireland. Here is also a small bust of Mr Henry Hunt, formerly of Northampton, a provincial statuary of some celebrity, and a pupil of Grinling Gibbons. Upper Drawing Room. Jane Skipworth, wife of Sir William Samwell, *Janssen.*

Upton Hall still contains some of the finest Rococo plasterwork that can be found in any Stately home attributed to Giuseppe Artari. It was commissioned in 1737, probably by James Gibbs the Architect. The Statue of Apollo is signed by Artari. The coats of arms of the Samwells, heads of Roman gods etc. are rare and beautiful, a reminder of graceful living.

The Samwells of Upton

The foundation of the family fortunes was laid by Francis Samwell, son of Richard Samwell, Esq., of Cottesford, co. Oxon., and a descendant of an old family of that name, long settled in Cornwall. Francis Samwell was auditor to King Henry VIII and Queen Elizabeth, and appears to have profited very considerably by the suppression of the religious houses and guilds of Northampton. He died in December, 1585, and was buried in the chancel of the church of All Saints, Northampton.

Sir Francis came from Cottesford. He purchased from the Crown a large part of the abandoned St. James Abbey land after its dissolution ending the 300 years of the Augustinian Abbey. He purchased the Manor of Rothersthorpe and it is thought he lived at the old Manor House in the Northampton Road. The capital letters F.S. 1579 are still to be seen on the medieval pulpit of Rothersthorpe church.

Sir Francis Samwell was laid to rest in All Saints Church in the crypt but owing to the great fire of Northampton in 1675 no trace was found afterwards of the monumental tomb also placed in the Church to his memory. After the fire large sums of money were given to the town Church by the county gentry. Among the distinguished names on the benefactor's board near the gallery steps is that of Sir William Samwell his son.

Some years ago I visited Cottesford to trace the house of the Samwells and the old Manor is still there. John Samwell purchased it in 1469 and the family is commemorated by a fine brass plaque on the south wall of the Church depicting John and his wife and their 15 children. The visit to Cottesford was made so enjoyable having walked straight into Flora Thompson's book "Larkrise to Candleford" with its fascinating reading of country people of her childhood. Cottesford is "Fordlow", Juniper "Larkrise", Fringford "Candleford Green."

Sir William Samwell, the eldest son, was, like his father, auditor to Queen Elizabeth, and received the honour of knighthood at the coronation of King James I. He was one of those "who contributed to the defence of his Country at the time of the Spanish invasion in 1588," the actual sum given by him being £25. In May, 1600, he purchased the manor of Upton which for upwards of two centuries continued to be the principal

Upton Hall. The dummy 3rd story added in the 17th century. Complete with walled windows.

Bradden, Northants. Home at one time of the Watson family who in the early 19th century claimed the Upon estate.

Nice view of gracious living in Samwell times.

One of the four seasons statues in the half round niches built into the hall frontage of Upton Hall.

The grand heavy oak entrance door bedecked with the century-old *Magnolia grandiflora*.

1965. Outside the main hall entrance. This old magnolia carries a flower most of the year.

seat of the family of Samwell. He was sheriff of Northamptonshire in 1607. He died January 23rd, 1627, and was buried in Upton Church. Sir William Samwell married Jane, daughter of Henry Skipworth, of Keythorp, Leicester, by whom he had four sons and two daughters.

A survey of the Manor of Kingsthorpe was made on 16th of April in the year of the reign of our Sovereign King James by the "Grace of God King of England, France and Ireland and Scotland"

by William Samwell   –   Knight
    William Tak   –   Knight
    John Henry   –   Esquire
    Thomas Mulso   –   Esquire
    William Blake   –   Gentleman

"by virtue Commissioners for the King to assess the total value of land to determine their right correctly conveyed and on oath to establish their right to the name place"

(List of names
(Individuals, location, nature of land houses etc. –
(Annual fee due to the Manor

Sir Richard Samwell was born 1599. He was sheriff of Northamptonshire in 1634. His father purchased Gayton Manor in 1607 from the Tanfield family. This lovely Elizabethian House is built as a crucifix and has a commanding view of Upper Nene Valley, and during the 200 years of the Samwells families was the home of the heir apparent.

He appears to have often resided there, for the Gayton parish registers contain numerous references to his family. Among them is a dispensation to eat meat during Lent, which shows that the Lenten fast was still strictly enforced in the days of the Stuarts.

A contemporary writer, who, speaking of the poverty of the vicarage of Rothersthorpe, of which church the Samwells were patrons, says:– "The Parsonage House and Glebe which by right of the old indowment (which lately remained upon record) doth belong to the vicar, is detained by Sir Richard Samwell, Knight, not by any good title in law, but some colour of an order (as a reported) in the exchequer, made long ago, when his grandfather perhaps was an auditor in th'exchequer, and so might procure some favour there in his owne behalfe, more than a poore miserable vicar could ever get reversed or altered. The tithe corn is worth one hundred pounds yearly, which also Sir Richard Samwell holdeth an appropriation. By this means the vicar is very poore, and in part scandalous, being a man chosen by Sir William Samwell, and there presented; who would be sure to place one in the vicarage that for want of wit and meanes should never be able to make any question of the parsonage House and Glebe. The want of bread and drinke in his own house, doth make him too often frequent the ale house, where if he talk foolishly, it is not much to be wondered at." On the outbreak of the Civil War in 1642, Sir Richard Samwell espoused the cause of Parliament, and in the following year was appointed one of the sequestrators for the county of Northampton, charged with the duty of seizing the property of all "notorious delinquents" who have "aided or should aid, opposition to the forces of Parliament." His method of dealing with "delinquents" is well illustrated by the case of George Preston, vicar of Rothersthorpe by a writer of that time.

Sir R[ichard] S[amwell], a bitter enemy at the clergy, sent a party of soldiers for him (and of all the days of the year, chose Easter day for this good deed) who seized him as he came out of the church after evening Sermon: and not suffering him to go home to his house to put off his gown, hurried him to Northampton gaol. He had then seven children, and his poor wife made earnest instances for his liberty, which some of the committee were willing to grant; but his patron, Sir R[ichard] S[amwell] (for he had the presentation of Thrup, and himself presented Mr Preston to it) was his enemy, and would not allow it. Neither was this: For the parishioners being tenants of Sir R[ichard] S[amwell], he ordered them not to pay their Tithes to Mr Preston. Upon which his wife and children came into a very desolate and forlorn condition. Neither did his malice stop here: For by extremity, want of changing, diet, and all necessaries (more than what his wife's mother sent him), Mr Preston, as well he might, fell sick: And though the jaylor acquainted the committee and Sir R[ichard] S[amwell] in particular of it; and though the Governor of Banbury offered to exchange four soldiers for him, yet would not Sir R[ichard] S[amwell] suffer him to be released, but kept him there till Michaelmas, when in plain words, he perished outright: having never been able to obtain his release from Northampton prison until God was pleased to deliver him at the same time from that and the prison of his body together: So that, as Mr Stephens justly observed, Sir R[ichard] S[amwell] in the sight of God and man murdered him. At the time of his death, he left his widow and seven children in a miserable condition; insomuch that the poor woman was forced by hard shifts and labours to support both herself and them. Sir Richard died in 1668, and was buried at Upton.

His son Sir Thomas Samwell was made a Baronet by Charles 2nd in 1675. He was M.P. for Northamptonshire 1683 to 1688 and M.P. for Northampton from 1689 to 1694 and while in office his name was associated with working conditions regarding the law of the land among Artificer Craftsman Labourers Men & Maid Servers, by the magistrates at the Quarter Sessions of April 1688. In the old Courthouse buildings in George Row Northampton are 2 full length portraits of William and Mary in his capacity as justice of the Peace and two other officials were appointed to commission one of the finest English portrait painters. He died 1693.

His son Thomas Samwell 2nd Baronet was born in 1687 and so was only 6 at his father's death but lived to be 34. He spent large sums of money on the Hall and Estate. He was M.P. for Coventry 1714 – 1722. In 1754 he held a commission in a regiment raised on behalf of King George. He died and like his father was buried at Upton.

The 3rd Baronet (1757-1779) again Sir Thomas son and grandson of the same name was unmarried and the title passed to his stepbrother Sir Wenman 4th Baronet, who after only another ten years died without issue.

NORTHAMPTON MERCURY

"His Grace the Duke of Grafton having appointed THOMAS SAMWELL, of Upton efg; to be his Gamekeeper for the Manours of Stoke-Bruern, Shutlanger, Ashton, Hartwell Road, and Blisworth; this is to give Notice to all Poachers; and unqualified Persons who shall be found Courting, Shooting, or otherwise defroying the Game within the said Manours, that (by his Grace's Orders) they will be prosecuted with the utmost Severity as the Law directs."

NORTHAMPTON MERCURY

SIR THOMAS WINE MERCHANT

Northampton, March 3, 1766.
    NOTICE is hereby given,
that Sir Thomas Samwell, Bart since the Death of his said Partner Mr. John Hopper, having entered into Partnership with Captain JOHN WYE, a Native of Oporto, whole Father, Brother, and other near Relations have long been, and now are, Members of the British Factory there, and who is master of the Ship Ann, constantly employed in the Trade to that Part: All Nobleman, Gentleman, and Others, may therefore depend upon being furnished with the very best WINES, of the choice(t) vintages, perfectly neat as imported by the ipe or in smaller Quantities, at their Wine-Vaults in the Town of Northampton; or to be delivered in any Part of this or the adjacent Counties, as shall be ordered, Sir Thomas Farmwell and Wye.

xtracts from the "Northampton Mercury" of October 24th 1769 and March 1831.

SAMWELL OBITUARIES

DIED. On Sunday last at Four in the Afternoon, after a lingering illness, at his seat at Upton Hall, near this Town. Sir Wenman Samwell, Bart, universally regretted. He was the last Baronet of that very ancient and respectable Family and was justly esteemed for the integrity of his Heart and the simplicity of his Manners. Leaving no issue, the Estates descend to his Nephew, T. S. Watson, Esq.

On the decease of Sir Wenman in 1789, the family estates devolved under the limitations of the will of Sir Thomas the third Baronet, to his nephew Mr. Watson, who adopted the name and arms of Samwell, by Act of Parliament in the following year. A pedigree of the family will be found in Baker's History of Northamptonshire, vol 1, p.224. In the early part of his life Mr Samwell was in the army, and for several years in active service in America and the West Indies. Whilst attached to the 15th foot, he was taken prisoner at St. Eustatia. After his return to England, he was, in 1803, appointed to Lieut-Col. of the old Northamptonshire militia, and in 1813 Lieut.-Col. commandant of the central regiment of Northamptonshire Local Militia. Few persons have passed a more active and useful life, being always ready to afford his services at the call of his country and his friends, and ever accessible to persons of all ranks. He married at St. Kitt's, April 15, 1780, Frances, second daughter of the Rev. Ren. Seymour Perfect; but, having had no issue, is succeeded in his estates by his next brother, Wenman Langham Watson Samwell, Esq. His remains were deposited in the family vault at Upton.

At the west end of this church there are four hatchments. On the south side of the nave are those of 1694, 1779 and 1789, and on the north side that of 1757.

Sir Thomas Samwell, Baronet
A.D. 1694

On a knight's helm, the Crest. On a coronet or, a squirrel sejant gules, cracking a nut proper. In a shaped shield, the Arms. Per pale, Dexter, Ermine, two squirrels sejant addorsed cracking nuts gules, Ulster hand on canton in chief, for Samwell.

Sinister, Sable, a cross of fusils or, over all a bend ermine, for Godschalk. Motto. In coelo quies. Background. Dexter black, sinister white. Thomas Samwell was the eldest son of Richard Samwell of Upton and Gayton. Esquire, by Frances, eldest daughter and co-heiress of Thomas, Viscount Wenman. He was created a Baronet the 27th December, 1675 and was Member of Parliament for the county of Northampton 1683-88 and for the Borough of Northampton from 1689 until his death. Sir Thomas married first Elizabeth the daughter and heiress of George Gorlay of Bower Hall, co. Essex, Esquire, by whom he had two daughters and after her death he married Anne, the daughter and heiress of John Godschalk of Atherston co. Warwick, in 1685, and by her he had one son, his successor, and two daughters. He died and was buried at Upton, on the 3rd March 1693-4. Baronet on the death of his father, in 1694, Sir Thomas in 1710 married for his first wife, Millicent, daughter and heiress of the Rev. Thomas Fuller, by whom he had two sons and four daughters. She died in May, 1716, and was buried at Upton. He married for his second wife, Mary, daughter of Sir Gilbert Clarke, in 1721, and by her he had one son and two daughters. From 1714 until 1722 he was a member of Parliament for Coventry. Sir Thomas died at Braddon, on the 16th November, 1757, and his widow died the 1st August, 1758, and they were both buried at Upton.

(Northampton & Oakham Archaeological Soc.)

Sir Thomas Samwell, Baronet
A. D. 1757

Crest on Baronet's helm, as before. In shapened shield, Arms. Per pale. Dexter. Samwell. Sinister. Azure. three escallops or, between two flaunches ermine, for Clarke. Mantling. Gules doubled argent. Ornamental border of leaves, with palm branches crossed beneath shield. Background. Dexter black, sinister white. Thomas Samwell, the only son of the before mentioned Sir Thomas Samwell.

Sir Thomas Samwell, Baronet
A. D. 1779

Crest on baronet's helm, as before. In ornamental shield, the Arms. Samwell. Motto. Christus sit regula vitae. Background. All black. Thomas Samwell, the eldest son of the before mentioned Sir Thomas Samwell by his first wife Millicent, was born in 1711, and on the death of his father in 1757, he became third Baronet. He was never married, and died on the 3rd December, 1779, and was also buried at Upton.

Elizabeth, Lady Samwell
A. D. 1789

Crest as before, in plain shield, the Arms. Per pale. Dexter. Ermine, two squirrels sejant two bars wavy ermine, on a chief of the field, a demi lion rampant sable, for Smith. Motto. Resurgam. A cherub's head at each angle of the shield, and branches of leaves on each side; death's head in base. Background. Dexter white, sinister black. Wenman Samwell, the eldest son of the last mentioned Sir Thomas Samwell, by his second wife, Mary, was born in 1728, and married Elizabeth, daughter of Thomas Smith, of East Haddon. On the death of his half brother, in 1779, he succeeded as the fourth and was the last Baronet. Lady Samwell, to whose memory this hatchment was made, died on the 28th June, 1789, without leaving issue, and Sir Wenman died on the 18th October, the same year, and they likewise were buried at Upton.

T.S.W. Samwell, Esq. OBITUARY in Gentlemans Magazine March 1831. Jan 15. At Upton Hall, near Northampton, Thomas Samwell Watson Samwell Esq. for upwards of forty years one of His Majesty's acting Justices of the Peace for the county, a Deputy-Lieut., and Verdurer of Whittlebury Forest. He was the eldest son of Thos. Atherton Watson, Esq. of Bedlinton in Northumberland, by Catherine, daughter, of Sir Thomas Samwell, the second Baronet of Upton, (and his second wife Mary, daughter of Sir Gilbert Clarke, of Chilcot in Derbyshire), and sister and heiress to Sir Wenman Samwell, the 4th and last Baronet.

Thomas Samwell Watson Samwell died without issue and was succeeded by his brother Wenman Langham Watson who assumed the arms and surname of Samwell. He died 1841 at the age of 81 and was buried with his forbears in the vault under the Chancel at Upton Church. This was then sealed.

After Wenman Langham Watson-Samwell died without issue in 1841, distant relatives contended for the property until 1881, and as the estate was insolvent, the whole acreage of Berrywood Farm was sold in 1874 for a lunatic asylum. Harry Bray the head gardener, whose father before him served in the same capacity, told me such was the neglect of the property that nettles grew out of the windows of Park House and Ivy covered the small Church of St. Michaels. At last after the church had been closed for a long time and various distant relatives occupied the house the whole estate was sold to Mr Turner of Northampton during the estate's long interregnum with no direct heir.

The medieval stone part of the house, altered probably by the Samwells in the early 19th Century, contains the old monk's room with its small monastic window. Many years ago the author, after being cautioned by the school, climbed old stairs and ladders to the room. All the floor boards were rotten and I carefully picked my way across the floor's cross timbers to the old fireplace end window of long ago. Many a protestant family gave shelter to a catholic relative in King James I time. The Regency south front with the coats of Arms high in the windows is probably the work of Samwell Watson of the Dower House in Duston, which has an identical west front and cast iron down pipes with the same date and initials T.S.W.S. The brick front (or brick tiling) was very fashionable then. The very nice 4 niches depicting the 4 seasons add delightfully to it. Also I must mention the glorious *Magnolia grandiflora,* which throughout the year always has a flower in bloom. Around the older parts of the house I am sure there were many old escape tunnels. Some years ago a gardener was scything when suddenly he fell down some 4ft into a large hole. His scythe fell across the entrance and saved him. Apparently the hole was quickly filled in and that was the last I heard of the story.

"JAMES HARRINGTON, a political writer of the 17th century, was born at the Manor House, Upton near Harpole, 1611. He was educated at Trinity College, Oxford, and after graduating he proceeded on a tour through Europe. He returned, however, before the outbreak of the civil war between the Royalists and the Roundheads. He allied himself to the Parliamentary forces and fought in several engagements. His adherence, however, appears to have been of a monetary description, and finding there was an opportunity for promoting his own interests in the opposite camp he abandoned the Roundhead and became an attendant upon the King himself, a personal attachment by the former to attend him on the scaffold. From subsequent events, however, it was shown that in abandoning the Roundheads he did not forsake their principles. He merely kept them out of sight, and after the King's death he again showed himself in his true colours. His early political opinions were stated in a Romance, 'The Commonwealth of Oceana', in which he advocated a system of Republicanism and ridiculed Monarchial government. The work is dedicated to Oliver Cromwell, and created as might well be imagined great interest and innumerable controversies arose from it. The principles advanced were to a great extent novel, though later years have seen them put in practice, in some cases with success and in others with failure. The Royalist party attacked the work with vehemence, while the Roundheads and Puritans were equally ardent in defending it. The result of the public discussion was to bring out in strong relief the fact that there were large numbers of men in the country who were imbued with the principles of republicanism. Some of these were called together in London, and a society pledged to support Republican principles was established. It was called the Rota, and it met every night at an inn, in London. The society discussed the chief political questions of the day. The action of the Government was carefully canvassed and current European politics also received attention. The result of those discussions was that a scheme of government by a Republic was drawn up, which provided for the due election of a Republican administration, one third of the members retiring by rotation every year, and every ninth year the whole body should be entirely renewed. Harrington carried his political opinions to such undue extremes that he was at length arrested on a charge of treason, and sent to the Tower, and then to St. Nicholas Island, near Plymouth but was shortly afterwards released on bail.

His first wife was Jane Samwell. He entered Trinity College, Oxford, as a gentleman Commoner in 1629, but left without a degree. After the death of his father, his grandmother, Lady Samwell, took James as her ward.

As a young man he travelled around in Holland and France, to Rome, where it is said he refused to kiss the Pope's toe, to Venice and back to England where he devoted himself to the education of his younger brother and two sisters. With Sir Thomas Herbert he attended Charles I as a groom of the bedchamber, and although he played no active part in civil war, he was with Charles on the Isle of Wight and accompanied him to Hurst Castle. Republican in principle, he seems nevertheless to have been devoted to the King and was deeply shocked by his death.

In 1656 Harrington published 'The Commonwealth of Oceana', expounding his own political theories in an imaginary history of Oceana (England) in which Olphaus Megalitor (Oliver Cromwell) set up the constitution of a new republic. His reference to contemporary affairs was so thinly disguised that the book stirred up an immediate controversy and was both attacked and defended in a series of pamphlets for several years. With the Restoration he was arrested and committed to the Tower on the charge of having attempted to change the form of government. His two sisters had petitioned for a trial when he was abruptly sent off to St. Nicholas Island in Plymouth Harbour. Later he was allowed to live in Plymouth and seems to have received lenient treatment, but unfortunately on the advice of a Dr. Dunston, he took heavy doses of guaiacum, which so injured his nervous system that he never really recovered. He died at Westminster in his sixty-sixth year, leaving a widow whom he had married late in life. "Serjeantson"

This charming letter, written by Derek Morrison, depicts those years of neglect after the death of the last of the direct line of the Samwells.

"I determined to go one fine day, with a determination to explore the mysterious region, when wiseacres assured me I should not find. Upton is situated about two miles from Northampton. It is not a village, but rather a hamlet, though I only know of two houses in the place. It seems to derive its name from Upton-Hall, a large mansion formerly the seat of the Samwell family, but now alas! shorn of its former glory. Now for my ramble, a pleasant walk about twenty minutes after leaving Duston toll-gate brings the traveller to Upton-Park. I must confess a shade of sadness on looking through the iron gates of the principal entrance to the grounds. A solemn-looking avenue of a species of pinus leads up to the mansion, now forsaken and desolate. Years have elapsed since those gates were opened to receive a carriage; indeed those sad, sombre-looking trees remind one of the cypresses planted in a graveyard, so silent is the spot, and so utterly forsaken by every living being. Shortly after passing the park entrance we come upon a little postern in the wall; this we open, and immediately find ourselves in a perfect Arcadia of loveliness-neglected and wild, but with that peculiar charm which English scenery always possesses; lilac and laburnam mingle their grace. There is a very curious tomb on the right side of the path on entering the churchyard; it is overgrown with ivy which conceals its shape, and all my endeavours to learn anything about it were unsuccessful. Perhaps your readers can give some information respecting it, for it looks as though a tale were attached to it. In conclusion I would advise the poet and the painter to visit Upton, and those who like the writer neither, will never repent a visit to this lovely spot, but well I am convinced, return home with a yet more passionate love for their beautiful and matchless fatherland. What other country can boast such lovely scenery as that of our own midland counties? True, it is said to be "tame", but what of that? Are not our verdant meadows, waving cornfields, luxuriant trees, and gently-flowing rivers more beautiful to the eye of him who loves his fellow-men than the bare rocks, foaming torrents, and general desolation of the north? These latter are suited to the misanthrope, who fancies himself-disgusted with the human race, but they who love their kind and are proud of the prosperity of their country will never cease to admire the beauty of our rich agricultural counties, with their gently undulating surface, presenting no harsh or inharmonious features to the view, but where every object joins in one glorious anthem to the great Creator who has given us all things richly to enjoy.

(*Northampton Express*, 1980)

Mr. Turner of Upton Hall

The new owner Mr. George Turner was for many years one of the active partners in the firm of Turner Bros., Hyde and Co, Campbell Square, Northampton. He was one of the original members of the firm but on a dissolution of partnership he retired from active participation in the business of the firm. In the meantime Mr. Turner had bought the Upton Hall Estate and went to reside in the ancestral home of the Samwells. There he busied himself chiefly in quiet agricultural pursuits. He was a keen huntsman, and was highly esteemed by many members of the Pytchley, the meets which he generally attended. In 1859 and at the time of his retirement, he had attained the rank of Honorary Major in Northampton Army Volunteers and had gained the esteem of his brother officers and men alike. He was placed on the Commission of the Peace for Northamptonshire by Earl Spencer, the Lord Lieutenant of the county and was a regular attendant on the Bench of the Northampton Divisional Sessions. He maintained unswervingly his adherence to the Liberal cause. He died in October 1892 and is buried at Upton with his wife who lived there until 1916.

1892 – The Will of George Turner Esq. J.P.

The will of George Turner, Esq, J.P., formerly of the town of Northampton shoe manufacturer, but late of Upton Hall near Northampton, was proved in the Northampton District Registry on the 4th February, by his sons, Charles Simkin Turner and Thomas George Turner, who are appointed executors. The personalty was sworn at £78,887 9s gross, and £78,123 16s 3d nett. He bequeathes his household furniture etc, to his wife absolutely, the same to form part of her third of his estate. He further bequeathes £1,000 to his nephew, John Nipper Turner; £500 each to his nieces, Elizabeth Robinson, Isabel Tebbutt, and Clara Turner; £50 to Elizabeth Turner, widow of his brother, John Turner; £200 to George Butcher, his clerk; £50 to each of the children of his brother Richard as an expression of his affection for them; £100 to the Northampton General Infirmary; £20 to each of his gardeners, John and William Bray; £10 to his groom, Anderson; and £10 to each of his domestic servants who had been five years or upwards in his service, all free of legacy duty. He further devises that his trustees are to pay to his wife one third of the residue of the rents etc. and after setting apart sufficient real or personal estate to secure his wife's income and the annuities, to apply the same unto and equally between his sons, Charles Simkin Turner and Thomas George Turner.

(Northampton Mercury)

1893 – Mrs. Turner of Upton Hall

To record the decease on Wednesday last Mrs. Mary Ann Turner, of Upton Hall. Wife of the late Alderman George Turner, J. P. former Mayor of Northampton. A daughter of Mr. J. Simkin, of Shropshire, she was married to Alderman Turner who died in October, 1892. She has resided at Upton Hall since and it is a matter of interest that it was there in March 1898 that led to the arrest of the most notorious housebreakers when being conveyed to London in a cab. They shot Inspector Hooper, of Northamptonshire County Police. For this murderous attack he was given penal servitude for life. Mrs. Turner has lived a retired life at Upton, and very many will miss her from their midst. Mrs. Turner leaves two sons Colonel C. S. Turner of Hardingstone, T. G. Turner, an active partner in the Turner Bros. Hyde and Co.

(Northampton Mercury)

1893

William Hudson bought Upton Estate in 1893 and wintered here and spent the rest of the year at Cheadle Hulme Hall in Cheshire (now part of Stockport). Wealthy like Mr. Turner, previous owner of Upton he was a partner in a large shipping company based in Manchester. He quickly set about rebuilding a lot of the Estate including the old stable block, coach house, and a new sewer system for the Hall. He rebuilt new cottages for the families on the farms of Spokes, some at Still's Farm and greatly improved the Church. Fetes are still remembered on the lawns by a few people now in their 90's. Sums of £100 or more were raised for St. Michael's Church, largely with the help of St. Peter's, Northampton members who faithfully worshipped together at Upton. Some came by pony trap, some walked to help their smaller daughter church raise funds etc.

Mr. Hudson died on April 13th 1916. Mrs. Hudson lived on at Upton Hall until 1935. The writer just remembers her being taken round the gardens in a wicker chair on wheels. Mr. James, her unmarried brother came to share the hall with her on the death of Mr. Hudson and he being the only relative resided there until his death in September 1946. So ended the house in private ownership. All the removable contents of the house were sold in a huge seven-day sale at the house stripped of its contents. The house and estate was sold to John Whites Trust. Soon the Hall became a private school. Today it is the home of Quinton House School.

1965

The beautiful plaster figures over the fireplace in the saloon at Upton Hall.

1965

The late Mr. and Mrs. Waddington in their cottage at Harpole. Both lived and worked in the Hall for many years, until it was sold in 1945.

1888

Turners Shoe Factory on the
mounts.

Shortly before the old Turners
Shoe Factory was demolished.

1909

Outside the main entrance to
the House

(left to right) Mr. James,
(lady unknown), Mrs. Hudson,
Mr. Hudson.

The Hudson's northern home at Cheadle (then in Cheshire), now a convalescent home.

1918

Mrs. Hudson seated outside Upton Hall.

1959

One of Mrs. Hudson's favourite trees. This fine pendulous Wych Elm on the lawns at Upton is now almost destroyed owing to Dutch Elm disease.

1945

Catalogue cover of the seven day sale of the hall contents.

1945

Mr. James, the last private owner of Upton Hall,
at the death of Mrs. Hudson (his sister).

Tithes and Upton

Copy of the letter of 1931 regarding the inability of the authority to determine the unpopular titheing and to extract the sum due to the Bounty from the parish of Upton office. The letter is sent to the incumbent of the Church, Rev. E. V. Martin.

Bounty Office
3 Deans Yard
Westminster SW1

29th September 1931

Dear Sir

Tithe Act, 1925
Northampton St. Peters, W. Upton 1. C.7/5827.

I am in receipt of your letter of the 23rd instant, and note that as a first step towards keying up the tithe collection list with the Apportionment and Map you will see Mrs. Hudson with a view to obtaining access to the documents in her possession.

If it seems to you that the documents which Mrs. Hudson has are the certified local copies of the apportionment and Map which were originally deposited, and should still be in the custody of the incumbent and churchwardens, you may perhaps find it possible to induce Mrs. Hudson to transfer them into the proper custody.

It is, of course, possible that the copies in her possession are private copies to which she has a perfect right, and that the copies originally deposited with the incumbent and churchwardens have been lost.

(2) Berry Wood Mental Hospital Committee pays £96.4.7. commuted tithe rent charge according to the collection list. According to your list of field numbers field 1a, 3 to 9 and 11 to 14 belong to the Hospital, the tithe rent charge on these fields being £82.14.4. A proportion amounting to £11.10.5. is also payable with respect to field no. 27 (the balance after deducting the proportion payable to Mrs. Hudson) leaving £1.19.10. with respect to the remaining property. The only property left however is a part of field no. 1, the entire rentcharge upon which amounts to only £1.9.1. and it seems clear that an over collection is being made in this case. Considerably less than half field no. 1 is owned by the Hospital and if an informal apportionment has been recognised the amount now payable by the Hospital Committee on an acreage basis is about 10/8d and the total tithe rentcharge payable would then be £94.15.5. which amount is made up as follows:-

Tithe Rentcharge on field, 3 to 9 and 11 to 14.	£82.14.4.
Proportion of tithe rentcharge on field no. 27.	£11.10.5.
Proportion of tithe rentcharge on field no. 1.	10.6.
	£94.15.5.

Estate carriageway from Weedon Road that once went to Berrywood Farm, the Dower House etc.

1969
Stable block, Upton.

1976

Elms sawn down on main drive (ravaged by Dutch Elm Disease).

1976

Old bridle path from Upton to Harpole.

From a painting (once in the Hall) of the old Sawyers buildings down Upton Mill Lane about 1870.

The old brick Dovecot on the west end of the Hall.

The Upton sand pit opposite Kitchen Gardens about 1880.

1965

Old Elms Drive to Upton alongside the A45 Weedon Road.

Sawing down the old estate drive to clear the site for the A45 dual carriageway.

Upton snowdrops.

Upton oilhouse (Lighting oil).

Upton stables.
Old coach entrance

Park House, at one time the
Dower House.

1960

Upton House Stables.

Homes of coachman and head gardener.

1960

A very large araucaria (monkey puzzle tree) in the lawns of Upton Hall.

Part Two – Upton Kitchen Gardens

The Greenhouses and Frames

The 100ft lean-to on to the high south wall was built in about the middle of the last century. Divided into two parts, one had 4 in. hot water pipes under the propagating benches and also enabled early potatoes to be grown in clay pots. These new potatoes were ready soon after Easter planted in January. The Royal Sovereign Strawberries in 4 in. pots (the runners were pegged into 3½ pots in the garden bed in the early summer) trailed down from the shelf, fruiting in early May to delight the ladies in the big house. Also in the warmer part of the lean-to, a section would be given over to large pots of Arum lilies to flower for Easter for the church. In the cooler part of the house were the vines. During the worst part of the winter all the trained branches were systematically pruned and brushed with a tar oil mixture (the open bark of the vine wood providing a host for all kinds of bugs, aphids, greenfly, whitefly, etc. Here and there on the whitewashed wall were the lovely old fragrant roses trained on wire frames, Orphelia, Madam Butterfly, etc.

It was fascinating to watch Harry Bray watering. All the rain water was collected in a large tank in the greenhouse (as was in my father's old nurseries) and the water used on the plants at the air temperature (some old private greenhouses even had a 4" hot water pipe go through the tank. Each plant would only have the amount of water it needed with a "Haws" watering can in his right hand and a 4ft cane with an old cotton reel on the end. He would tap each clay pot for sound: a hollow ring – a dry pot; a dull sound – needs no water.

Autumn with the main drives to the house carpeted with leaves, the paths round the lakes, the shrubberies all were kept clean from October until December and the leaves removed on a large two-wheel barrow and stacked in a large square heap in an adjoining pit across the Weedon Road (once a sand pit) for 12 months and then when rotted, brought back and dug in the gardens. Harry Bray, during the winter was also church warden at the church next to the kitchen gardens. On Saturday he would light the boiler in the church for the Sunday service. This old round boiler was 6ft down in the west end of the church. By removing the heavy iron grating one can still see what a task it was to wheel the solid fuel in. The system was simple. From the boiler a large wrought iron chimney (or flue) went some 2ft under the main aisle to the west end with gratings at intervals to emit warm air. Then a tall chimney on one side of the chancel drew the smoke and heat through the church. This system was used in early glasshouse heating, but with the boiler outside until the latter part of the 19th Century when hot water pipes were everywhere in use.

All the staff, from the boys (learners and the head gardener) would be attired in green beige aprons over their winter coats or summer shirts, clean blackened boots every morning, 7 till 5.30, Saturday till 12 pm. The head gardener never took his week's holiday. The only time he had away was as a young man when his father was head gardener and he volunteered in Northamptonshire yeomanry in the Boer War and later served in the 1914-18 war. The walls facing south and west were adorned with trained pears and plums. In winter you would find them pruning and tying the new branches to the wires. Later in the early summer, thinning the fruits so all were of the best quality to take up to the house.

It is some 60 years since I first opened the green door in the high stone wall of the kitchen gardens at Upton to fetch fresh spring cabbage for my father's shop in Alma Street, St. James. Like most private walled gardens in the early 1930s, produce was being sold as fewer servants were being employed in the large houses so less vegetables and fruit was needed. A few steps into what were beautiful gardens, I was quickly approached by the head gardener demanding to know what I was doing in there. The splendour of the endless rows of bush fruit, some were half standard red currants, white currants and gooseberries. The rows of successive sowings of culinary peas all neatly stuck with the traditional cob nut sticks. A row of this was grown in the orchard and a length was cut down each year for this purpose and also for besoms for the autumn leaf sweeping. Enormous crops of strawberries were grown "Royal Sovereign" and much better flavour than today's varieties and pink and gold in colour. Every new crop of strawberries planted in the ground was double dug. Old leaf mould and manure applied in the deep trench on the bottom.

1912

Hall Gardens, beautifully kept. Harry Bray was the head gardener.

1960

The old conservatory, one of the many neglected buildings in 1960.

1970

The kitchen gardens then let to Mr. Collett and partly restored.

Upton Kitchen Garden Conservatory

This large Victorian conservatory held an exotic array of pot plants of all kinds in the centre rows of staging surrounded by a flat bench of the same height covered by a slate bed. Either side hung a wooden slatted blind that was let down on summer days for shade. The entire floor was tastefully tiled. Outside the delightful protruding 2 door entrance was a large boot scraper for the gardeners. Opposite was a huge circular wrought iron pheasantry (still there). On the east wall was a small iron closure for rearing, all originally built for white pheasants. There was a long centre walk, once some 200ft. long, with a wrought iron pergola adorned with old varieties of scented climbing roses. It was indeed a great joy to walk through.

Heating

At the north side of the large lean-to greenhouse were the potting sheds, apple store etc., also the large coke boiler which had to be attended, with the awful choking smell of clinkers and ashes being removed in an enclosed pit. I can still remember vividly the stoker climbing back up the ladder gasping for air. This heating arrangement was not only for the greenhouses but was used to heat some 100ft of frame yard to the south of them. These old English frame beds with rows of 4" hot water pipes beneath some 18" of compost provided early crops of potatoes, lettuce, radishes etc. Later filled with cucumbers and tomatoes.

Pests and Diseases

You might ask the question "How did they cope with aphids, white-fly etc in their greenhouses? To begin with tar oil wash that was applied to the dormant vine wood in the winter. One deterrent was that the whole of the houses received a heavy spraying with Jeyes fluid watered down sufficiently to kill all bugs etc, then hosed down leaving the glass and woodwork bright and clean. So the greenhouses, and also all clay pots, canes and wooden seed boxes etc., were sterilised once a year.

Not so long ago a customer was walking out of our nurseries with an old heavy 10" clay or terracotta pot (We still use one hundred for Arum lilies) that had been mistakenly sold to her. She seemed delighted to have acquired this old "Sankey's Pot." I rather surprised her by telling her she had now acquired a collector's piece. The 4 acre walled garden was only entered by one pair of double doors (for a hand cart). The other door was at the Weedon Road entrance next to the second gardener's cottage which was pulled down for road widening many years ago. Close watch was kept on these doors. If found open for a short time a rabbit would find its way in. Pandemonium would set in if a rabbit was in the kitchen garden, and it would be found and shot. With pines and a heavily wooded area around, a 12 bore gun was always kept in the potting shed for use against incoming birds.

Squirrels especially were devastating among the glasshouse fruits, so much so that in the fruiting period fine mesh wire netting was placed over the greenhouse vents. One of the birds that caused so much trouble to garden peas etc., were jays. Years ago none of the gardens were netted but the troublesome birds were shot and hung high over the crops. This deterrent seemed to work and often entailed the gun being used at 4.30 on a summer morning.

The Water Supply

Upton Estate with its farms and fields was supplied with water from a spring at Lodge Farm pumped by an automatic ram on a hill. It was piped to the hall and to the lakes. A huge tank in the roof of Upton Hall was filled from an outside well providing the drinking water at tap pressure. Bob Webb was responsible as Estate man for all this. The 3 lakes were full of fish in my young days, kept completely clean from water weed and every year or so completely emptied by a drainage system, just a stone depression remaining in each lake to contain the fish while cleaning out proceeded. This process called for all the labour from the gardens to act quickly and get the work done. It was listening to the gardeners talking one day concerning this that my next story begins.

1939

May in the long lean-to green house with perennial wall geranium and scented Ophelia rose.

The old glasshouse and the frames smashed by hailstones in the summer of 1928.

1968

Another view of this fine old glasshouse built around 1840 with a tiled floor and roller blinds.

1975

The old pheasantry minus the outer wire netting, which now comes under a conservation order made some years ago. The Northampton Development Corporation restored the metalwork and it still stands in the Quinton House sports field.

Fishing

What little time I had from school after helping my father (all boys had a job in those days helping tradesmen before and after school) was spent fishing in the summer down at Upton Mill. After repeatedly being asked by the gardeners how many I had caught, I resolved to do something about my repeated negative fishing exploits. So one Saturday morning I walked boldly through the boundary gate leading onto the main drive to the house whereupon a loud voice said "Where are you going?" I turned round as I lifted the latch on the gate and replied "I'm going to ask Mr. James if he will let me fish in the lakes". He said "He'll shoot yer!" But I carried on across the gravel drive nervously to the large oak front door and gently lifted the large iron door knocker awaiting my sentence. Footsteps seemed a long way off till the heavy door was opened and I was confronted by the Squire. Cap in hand I stood there. "Please Sir, I've come to ask you if you would let me fish in the lakes". He replied "You know nobody is allowed to fish there. You're Golby's boy, I've seen you in the gardens." Having surveyed me standing there as an intruder on sacred ground, he said "Alright you may come, but you must never bring anyone with you." This was in 1928. I was able to bring my mother a plate of fish back to cook, in those days a much needed addition for the table. So for many years as a boy, then as a young man I became very much attached to Upton, the perfection of growing and the help given to my father. The continuous journeys fetching surplus produce on a carrier bike to a house shop in Alma Street. The peace and tranquility, the quietness of the large house. As I sat there years ago the doves, the odd moorhen and pheasant, the voice in the distance calling the cows in for milking, the gentle clinking of the best china being prepared for tea. This wonderful undisturbed peaceful setting. Sadly time removed it all. The last of the Hudson family, Mr. James who claimed the estate from Mrs. Hudson (his sister) died in 1945. Only distant relatives remained in the house and all the contents were sold. The gardens were no more and the old glasshouses allowed to decay.

Mr. James' red marble tomb is in the south east corner of the churchyard in front of the large Hudson family grey granite tomb.

Harvest

Harvest time at Upton Church was a very special time for the gardeners. Wheelbarrows full of produce were taken there beginning on the Friday. All the window ledges were laid with fresh green moss, then the fruit and vegetables were placed on there. The finest bunch of grapes from the vinery were hung over the pulpit. The service in the afternoon would be joined by St. Peter's, the parent church. Every seat would be filled.

Bob Webb

Bob Webb was one of Northampton Saints' invitation players in the 1920s. The clubs hooker 1922 to 1929, he won two England caps in 1926, playing against Scotland, and another in 1929 playing against France. He lived in an estate cottage at Upton, and was responsible for the maintenance of all the estate property. His brother in law was 'Fanny' Walden, who after playing for Northampton Town Football Club joined Tottenham Hotspur. During the last world war Bob Webb served with the Royal Observer Corps, and in that capacity joined an American warship that took part in the invasion of 1944. He received the Royal Observer Corps long service medal to mark his retirement. His only son Robin keeps the electrical shop opposite Franklins Gardens.

Bob Webb, Saints and England rugby player.

Part Three – Upton Farms

Upton Mill

The Spokes family of Upton Mill commenced there in 1812. Some 7 generations have lived there since. In the time of William I it was Upton and was let at 12 shillings and sixpence a year. In 1086, it was described as a flour mill driven by water. By the time of Edward I, some 200 years later it was worth £15 a year .

Mr. Daniel Spokes was the first of the family to work the Mill. He came from Holcot in 1812 and this remarkable family of Millers were tenants of Holcot, Wilton, Weston (near Rugby) and Twyford Mills then. Upton Mill in 1812 was like so many village corn mills of only cottage size described as 10ft to the eaves, 16ft to the roof ridge of thatched straw. These old written bills are still in the hands of the present owners John Spokes. To Thomas Keffs of Kislingbury, one dated June 26th 1817 was for one sack of "second flour" £3-6s-8p. On the same account is "deduction of 7s for doing work at the Mill." Here is a description of the Mill at work then:-

The corn would have to be carried from the ground to the third storey, and from thence it would commence on its primitive journey. It would be shot into the garners, thence through the cleaning machine before it was precipitated between the stones and then out into a trough below, when it would be drawn up by means of a glaring driven by the mill and through the screen which supplied with brushes, brushed the flour through the sieves and so separated the flour from the pollards, it produced a flour coarser than the modern white, for the meshes through which it went were only of steel and not silk as today. This was the process with wheat flour, and the stones peculiar to wheat grinding were of a composite character, grooved in such a manner that as the wheat entered the centre it would be ground and carried to the outside of the stone and fall into the trough below. The barley grinders which ran in conjunction with the wheat stones were perfectly flat and the process finished at the grinding. Once the corn had gone through the Barley Stones and all gone through the hopper the leather was released, and loosing the bell, an iron spur on the revolving upright which turned the stone would strike the bell and warn the workman that was the end of that particular customer's lot, or would convey the information that the hopper required feeding again.

A similar device was operating on the wheat stones, though its structure was different. In this case a bottomless bowl was suspended over the sleeve down which ran the ground flour. So long as the bowl was full the wheat in the garner would be fed to the stones, but so soon as the flour had passed through, the bowl would spring up and cause the feed of the hopper to become enlarged. If no further wheat came down it was the signal that the parcel of that particular customer had been completed, and the flour was there upon drawn up again to go through its further process before being finally placed in its sack for delivery later on.

Upton Mill and House bedecked with Virginia Creeper, an early autumn scene. Part of the disused Mill is said to date from Norman times.

The old Mill had an output of 6 sacks of flour per day. It was always at work grinding small quantities for the village labourers, especially gleaned corn. This was called "gristing". This would be used by the housewife and baked into bread, sometimes the small holder would want a few sacks of corn ground or a horse and cart would go round the parish collecting a mixed load for grinding, so all this brought "Grist to the Mill".

The Miller was paid 6d per bushel for grinding barley, and the Miller kept the offals.

Over the East entrance doorway of the adjoining Mill House is a datestone and the initials T.S.W.S. (Thomas Samwell Watson Samwell), and it was at this time that the Victorian restoration of the Mill & House took place. At that time a New Water Wheel was installed of 14 feet in diameter and the cost amounted to a total of £48. Wonderful workmanship was shown by the skilled carpenters working in hardwoods oak, elm, ash, and surprisingly apple wood was used in hard bearing shafts supporting the revolving stones. This particular Mill wheel ran almost continuously for 50 years until 1900 when the Mill closed. By then steam was being installed into the larger Mills. Corn was being ground by factory town Mills, not reliant on water power and these could run continuously winter and summer. A hundred years ago over a quarter of an acre of Mill Pond was essential to hold precious water up in a dry summer. Like other similar sites they are no more.

Various members of the family since 1812 have held high office in Public Services. For example, John Spokes served on the Highways Board before the Rural District Council was formed and was the first representative for the parish on the old board of Guardians and later Chairman of the newly formed District Council. W. B. Spokes, the present owner's great grandfather succeeded his father on the Council and in later life was chairman of Northamptonshire County Council and a magistrate. Although milling is now long forgotten, several hundred acres are owned and rented by the family. Home Farm, the first buildings down Upton Lane, was the private farm of Upton Hall, supplying all the needs of the family and staff of the big house until 1945.

Upton Hall Farm

The Boswell family appear to have farmed Hall Farm in the first half of the 19th Century. The tombstones in Upton churchyard tell us H. Boswell died in 1841 and his son died in 1876.

Harry Havil Still, who still lived in Abbey Park Terrace by 1898 rented some of the land of this farm. His brother Tom's butchers shop was in the busy shopping area then of Marefair and his mother Clara owned a dairy next door. Both properties, numbers 6 and 7, are now almost at the corner of Horseshoe Street (owing to road widening).

Claude Still, Harry's son, began his career in the Army and later served in the Great War 1914-18 with the rank of Captain before the war ended.

The old road from near Kislingbury Bridge that went to Pineham Farm (buildings demolished some 60 years ago) then on to Upton Mill.

In 1923 Claude and his family were tenants of Bozenham Mill Farm near Grafton Regis. Then the family purchased a farm at Sawtry in Huntingdonshire (now in Cambridgeshire). By 1941 the family moved to Upton Hall Farm. Then his father retired to 44 Millway where he died in 1943.

Today Claude's son David lives at Hall Farm House, and his brother Miles resides at Harpole.

Miss Norris recalls her early days in Mr Still's cottages down Upton Lane. Her father, a farm labourer, lost an arm working among the cattle as a young man, then took to droving, driving cattle as far as Everdon from Bridge Street Station. One day he drove 200 pigs from the same station to Upton. Miss Norris' five brothers all worked for the Still Family on their farm at Upton after leaving school. Claude Still had butcher shops some 60 years ago, and she remembers the large barn at Park Farm being used as a slaughter house. She also remembers old Mr. Bray who looked after the white pheasants in the large circular pheasantry (still preserved in the old kitchen gardens). Also his son William Bray cleaning Mrs. Hudson's Rolls Royce in the entrance, to the stable yard. Her memory recalls Summer sunny afternoons when her parents took her through Upton Mill, on the road to Kislingbury, passing the old house and farm building of Pineham Farm (now demolished). Bert Westley the Duston postman, said if he only had half penny stamped letters for Upton he would leave them in his pocket assuming they were bills of no importance, and leave them for another day.

Upton Lodge Farm

William Facer and his son William farmed Lodge Farm from the beginning of the 19th century to 1850. Then the Farmer family were tenants. Afterwards came Edward Loake who died in 1876 and his sons who farmed till 1900 when Sam Spokes who, with his brother William were brought up at Upton Mill agreed between them at the vacancy of a tenant at Lodge Farm that Sam should apply for it, and this land is still farmed by the same family today.

Walter Spokes continued after his father Sam died. Graham (his son) today looks after a large dairy herd, nowadays so few milking herds remain that were once part of everyday country life.

Upton Park House

It is thought that Park House could well have been a Dower House of the Upton house in Samwell's time before Duston House was built in 1820.

Paths and drives show that they were part of the interconnecting continuity of the large hall.

Park House in the early 1920's became a private dwelling and the buildings in Park land were included in the tenancy of Hall Farm.

View of Park House from the park. The field in the foreground has an area of nettles denoting stone foundations of the old village in medieval times.

1930

Mr. and Mrs. Franklin Senior outside the cottage
down Upton Lane

1935

Last load for the day at Still's
Farm. Mr. Smart on the Rick.
Arthur Franklin on the ground.

1930

Mrs. Franklin and nephew outside their cottage at Upton Hall Farm.

1932

Ernie and Jack Franklin (in the background) at their Hall Farm Cottage.

Terisa Ross (from Upton Farm Cottages) and David Ryan's wedding at Upton Church.

1960

Upton Lodge Farm cottage. Family left to right:- Christine, John (Berry), Elizabeth, Winifred, Terisa, and Eileen.

1965

Work on the A45 dual carriageway outside the Upton Lodge Farm entrance.

1962

Elizabeth Ross with her father at her Upton Church wedding.

1956

Mr Ross came to work for Samuel Spokes in 1955. Seven children were raised in this small cottage, one of two that stood at the approach to the Lodge Farm. Sadly they were pulled down some 15 years ago. Here he is seen with some of his family outside the cottage.

Part Four – St. Michael's Parish Church, Upton

Introduction

A great deal of this History of Upton we owe to Robert Serjeantson whose researches were skilfully carried out almost a hundred years ago. Here is an appreciation of his work written recently by Dr. Sargant, Church Historian.

Robert Meyricke Serjeantson MA, FSA (1822-1891). Several of the rectors of St. Peter's have further distinguished themselves in the Church, for example as Archdeacons of Northampton, but only one became a mediaeval historian, Robert Serjeantson. Almost alone he established the church history of Northampton. Although he was always a busy and devoted parish priest, as curate of Holy Sepulchre, and then as rector of St Peter's and of St Michael, Upton, he wrote four major books, one about each of the ancient churches of Northampton, not to mention very many other works, on the castle, the religious houses and other aspects of the town's history. Admittedly he remained unmarried, but his studies involved research on a vast scale, visiting libraries in Oxford, Peterborough, London, Canterbury, or even Dublin. In such places he rediscovered the legend of St. Ragener. Yet his few surviving parishioners describe a conscientious and energetic pastor, beloved by everyone.

Today, St. Michael's Church, Upton is in the care of The Churches Conservation Trust. An Annual Service takes place at the end of September, together with a Harvest Festival celebration. Quinton House School uses the church for seasonal services for the children and help keep the church clean and tidy, and in an acceptable condition for visitors. The Church owes a debt of gratitude to the Venerable Basil Marsh (now retired), who formed the friends of Upton. He realised that one day this small church would be needed for the large expansion of West Northampton. So together we arrived at the decision to arrange all of the valuables of the church to be placed elsewhere, waiting to be returned when the doors again for the public worship.

Anglo Saxon Upton

In 1966 excavations were made west of Upton Church and like so many sisters of Norman churches earlier Saxon buildings have been found. Here at Upton the remains of what was thought to be a large weaving shed was discovered some 30ft long by 18ft wide. Extensive remains of supporting timbers were found. It was possible to excavate only the South and East of the building owing to the improvement of the A45 with road widening on the North side some years previously. The report of 1965 suggests the interior of the ends of the building were a good deal heavier than the sides. Also the structure was supported by an H timber construction which in the the centre carried a post to support the ridge pole. The walls showed no signs of having to carry a great weight with no trace of deep post holes. The whole would not have supported any great weight on the roof. Was it built only for a short duration?

(Northants Past & Present)

Upton Church

St. Michaels Church, Upton is an ancient building of local stone in the Norman and Early English styles built originally as a Lord of the Manor's private Chapel. Together with Kingsthorpe Church, these were for centuries, Chapels of Ease to St. Peter's, Northampton. Then in 1850 Kingsthorpe Church received its independence. Upton remained part of St. Peter's until 1966. The reader will realise turning over the pages of this Church's history how close was the band of friendship and worship of St. Michael's and St Peter's members.

The church was closed for almost 40 years until the restoration in the late 19th century, by then almost covered in ivy.

Some of the old dead ivy can still be seen today on the south side of the church.

Various Wills of 15th and 16th Century concerning Upton Church are interesting. John Stokes and William Else leaving their bodies to be buried in Upton Churchyard. In 1648 the tithes were valued at £60. On May 29th 1660 in honour of King Charles' restoration a special sermon was given to the clergy in charge for that day as follows:-

"A thanksgiving sermon for the Blessed Restoration of his sacred Majesty, Charles II. Preach'd at Upton before Sir Richard Samwell Knight, May 29th 1660. By William Towers, Bachelor in Divinity, eighteen years titular Prebendary of Peterburgh; sixteen, titular parson of Barnake. Now (by the friendly favor of Mr. Reynolds) continued curate at Upton, in the diocese of Peterburgh. With a short apostrophe to the King. London; Printed by R.D. for Thomas Rooks, at the Holy Lamb at the east end of St. Paul's, 1660."

Originally the Church roof was thatched, probably until the 15th Century. A much shallower pitched roof was later rebuilt raising the eaves, making the Church loftier and much easier to maintain some 100 years ago. On two occasions lead was stolen off the roof so the Diocese of Peterborough decided to remove the rest of it and replace with stainless steel with a soundproof underlay of plastic material.

Over the South Porch is the remains of the coat of arms of the Knightley family. V. K. (Valentine Knightley) 1574 probably when he added the Porch to the Church before he sold the estate to the Samwells in 1600. The stained glass east window dates from a restoration of the Chancel in 1850, although not completed until 1870 and is to the memory of Eliza Wickens of St. Peter's and contains a representation of the Crucifixion and also depicts the Passion. The previous east window was given to Wenham Langham Watson Samwell and probably carried no dedication and was placed there in 1797.

The north and south doorways have had overhead 3 stepped arches. The priests doorway having a 2 stepped arch. Mass dials can be found on old Churches like Upton on the South side where time could be measured by placing a piece of wood in the centre hole to let the sun cast its shadow on to the dials to indicate it was Mass time. One can be found at the Priest's door east side, another in the west wall and the other in the South Porch. It is my opinion that these were not always in the original setting, maybe through rebuilding or alterations. Mr. Ray Tricker of Redundant Churches writes that he thinks that in the late 1200 the nave was extended westwards and the two "lanet" windows were built into the West Wall.

The tower built onto the church is elegant, and embattled with two 14th century belfry windows. As one climbs the ancient sandstone steps curving your way up the small dusty staircase one finds oneself facing the old clock. The iron weights last a week from their high settings, falling down some 40ft to operate the clock, which has only one face fronting the front door of the hall. There are two buttresses to the tower.

The Church Fabric 1637

1637. King James I Commissioner's report of the condition of Upton Church (old English made readable for the author by Mrs. Minchinson of Northants Record Office.)

25 October 1631. Coram et Doctore Sibthorpe Comissionarus.

In the Chancell
There are two seates, the one on the southside and another on the north side which take up too much of the Chancel and that on the south side is undecent at the east end and clamped together with iron.

The ancient seates of the Chancell are removed upward on the north side by reason of one of the seates aforesaid and the said ancient seates are broke{n} and here it is an undecent bench or shale (?) layd upon certaine rough stone undecently dawbd together which are fitt to be amended or removed.

The Communion table is too long like a drinkeing boord and it is not cancell'd in which nevertheless might convenient{ly} be done by placing the Cancell against the middest of the monument and returinge it at at east end of the monument on the south side and proporconably at the north end and affixing a kneeling bench to which all the communicantes maie come up as they ought{e} and there reverently receive the sacrament kneeling. The windowe in the east end is partly broken in the glasse at the topp and dawbd up at the bottome.

The great east door unused since private ownership, some 50 years ago.

East windows from Ecton Church built into the gardens of the Hall by Cosfords (the church builders) in the late 19th century.

Over the south porch, where once was a sundial with the initials of Valentine Knightley.

The chancell doore is shattered and broken.

The pavement is undecent and uneven and is patch{ed} with undecent stone.

The tymber of the Chancell takes wett and the wa{lls} are staned in divers places.

The Church

The uppermost seat or pewe on the south sid{e} wantes boardinge in the bottome and is a foot too high.

The pavement of the Church is uneven and patch{ed} in divers places.

The North Church doore is annoyd with netl{e} weedes and rubbishe soe that the parishioners cann{ot} conveniently goe in and out at the same & the { } is partly rotted therewithall.

The South Church doore is partly rotten and broken {at} the bottome. The lower most seate < on the north and south side want boording i{n} {another} west but one on the north.

The seates belowe the crosse space on both sides want boording at the bottom & are broken.

The seat above the crosse space on the north side & the three first seates above the crosse space on the south side are undecently patched up with ashen boordes and unplained and noe waie aunanswerable either in stuffe or workemanship to the ancient seates of the church. And 3 of the said seates want boording in the bottome.

The walls are stained with rayne and filth in diverse places and the leades appeare to be of repaire.

The Font hath not <a> decent and convenient cover but like the cover of a powdering tubb.

3 Litle windows one at the west end, one in the porch and south stopped up.

They want a poore mans box.

The ministers pewe is not convenient for to read prayers reverently in which may be amending by adding part of that space hereto which is under the pulpit and by deskeinge of it east and west and it wantes boordinge in the bottome and the stepps into the pulpitt are dangerous and very inconvenient and the worke of the pulpit is broken in diveres places & it wantes paintinge & varnishing.

A windowe over the Church porch is stopped up with stone.

Bookes & Ornamentes
The bible is unsufficient and not of the nowe translacion but of a translacion in Henry the 8th tyme.

The Common Prayer book is not sufficient not accordinge to this majesties directions in the prayers for the Queene and royall progenie.
Jewell & Harding
Erasmus Paraphrase

God & the King
A book of straing preachers   } wantes
The table of degrees

There wantes a large flagon for the Communion.

Three little windows in the steeple viz.
One north one south & one west stopped up.

The Old Boilers

Beneath the carpet near the North door is the original iron grating. At the East end some 6ft down is the old solid fuel boiler which the head gardener used to light on the Saturday before the Sunday worship so that the initial dust and smoke would be gone and the building completely warm. At the West end of the Church a tall chimney drew the fumes and smoke through a round 10 in. wrought iron pipe from one end to the other. Also still near the old steps is a small stove in the north wall that warmed the Squires pew box. Both old boilers probably date from the early 19th Century when the same flue heating was used in the old greenhouses.

The Restoration of 1832

In the years 1832 and 1833 the interior of the parish church at Upton was repaired and beautified, when all the pews and wainscot in the church and chancel were varnished, the belfry enclosed with wainscotting, a new communion table added, all the monuments belonging to the Samwells restored, the church porch paved with freestone and ceiled, four stone pinnacles added to the tower, with new battlements and a new gilt vane, the outside of the church and chancel new pointed, and the ground of the churchyard levelled, all at the sole expense of the present proprietor of the estate, Wenham Langham Samwell, Esq.

CHARLES WEST, M.A. CURATE

The Restoration of 1894

Under the renowned architect Matthew Holding, Upton Church was restored. If one observes the south wall closely, traces of old dead ivy can be seen that completely covered the church. After 40 years of closure three Norman windows were found and reopened. Today the North Norman doorway us covered by a plain door for protection. This many times has been broken by thieves trying to enter. The large northern windows are of the perpendicular style and are subject to alterations of 1892. The south windows are similar except the ones that incorporate the stained glass of the benefactor. A small piscina is on the right side of the Chancel and also in the Sanctuary we find an Aumbrey. One old English window remains in the inner west wall, a reminder of a period before the Tower was built later in the 14th century. The priests door and a low window are in the South Chancel. A lot of the small panes of glass in the windows are typical of their period, not clear glass and sometimes a slightly pale colour.

I am indebted to Mr. Roy Tricker of The Churches Conservation Trust for his recent research into the Victorian alterations inside Upton Church for the following.

The church as in the time of private ownership.

The Victorian pulpit. Note the old stone steps that once led to the old rood cross. The fire grate for the squire's pew box. The plaster cast of St. Michael.

Samwell's Hatchment when placed at the rear of the organ pipes.

The alabaster recumbent figures are said to have had their fingers, toes and noses chopped off by the swords of Cromwell's men at the time of Naseby, having quartered their horses on the Earth floor of the church.

18th century old Upton Church English leather bound bible.

The Turners' Memorial tablet in Upton Church chancel.

IN MEMORY OF
CEORCE TURNER ESQ
OF UPTON HALL. J.P.
BORN 31ST OCT. 1833, DIED 13TH OCT. 1892

ALSO

MARY ANN TURNER,
WIFE OF THE ABOVE
BORN 6TH SEPT. 1834, DIED 5TH SEPT. 1900

What to see inside the Church

A *door*, fashioned in the 18th century, admits us to a colourful interior, full of character and interest. The *walls* were scraped of their plaster and their stonework exposed during the 1893 restoration. Of this date also are the shallowly-pitched tiebeam *roofs*, which are very worthy replacements of the 15th or early 16th century ones. In the. west walls, each side of the 14th century tower arch, are two tiny *openings* (a quatrefoil to the south and a cross-shape to the north), through which people could look into the church from the upper floors of the two *chambers* each side of the tower. Such chambers are uncommon, but not unique. It is thought that they had upper floors and maybe provided accommodation, when needed, for a priest or sexton. Beneath the southern quatrefoil is a rectangular opening, which is filled with 15th century *traceried woodwork* – possibly from the former rood screen or maybe even made especially for it.

The only evidence left of the rood and loft, which stood at the division of the nave and chancel, are the four steps of the *rood loft staircase*, which rise where the wall has been cut away beneath the Norman window on the north side of the nave and which gave access to the loft (or gallery) above the former screen, effectively lit, no doubt, by the window.

Three recesses may be seen in the chancel walls. On the south side of the sanctuary is what was probably a *piscina*, (although its drain has now gone) beneath a trefoil-headed arch. Beside it is a small opening which extends through the thickness of the wall. In the east wall is a rectangular *aumbry* (another may be seen in the north wall, behind the tomb), which was a cupboard for storing the Sacred Vessels.

Near the north doorway is a 17th century oak *chest*, where parish valuables and documents were stored. Near the south doorway is the 17th century *Communion Table*, which is served as the altar here, until the present altar arrived in 1907.

The 18th century font and the lectern are now at St. Mark's, Wellingborough and some of the nave benches are now in use at St. Benedict's Church, Hunsbury. The eight *nave benches* which remain have beautifully carved ends, with coats of arms. These were designed by Holding, as were the choir and clergy *stalls* (the latter with the arms of the Province of Canterbury and the Diocese of Peterborough), which were dedicated in 1899 and were made in oak by Mr. Henry Martin and carved by Mr. L. S. Reynolds of Northampton. They were Upton's memorial to Queen Victoria's Diamond Jubilee, thanks to generous donations by Mrs. Thomas of Upton Hall, and the Women's Guild of St. Peter's, Northampton, towards the clergy stalls.

Much of the 19th century work was designed by the Northampton architect, Matthew Holding who supervised the major restoration of the church in 1893. An earlier restoration was of the chancel, it took place in 1850 to the designs of Mr. Eden Law of Northampton. The communion rails, altar and Reredos, also the vestry screen, were added by Messrs Jones and Willis in 1907/8.

Chancel, north wall
1. A plaque tells us of 16th and 17th century members of the Samwell family, including Sir William, who purchased Upton,

2. Thomas Samwell Watson Samwell, J. P. (died 1831) has a plaque by Whiting of Northampton, with a long biography and an epitaph.

3. Wenman Langham Watson Samwell (died 1841), also by Whiting.

Chancel, east wall
4. Clarissa Woodford, grand-daughter of Sir Thomas Samwell (died 1846).

5. Catherine, daughter of Sir Thomas Samwell (died 1790) and her husband, Thomas Atherton Watson (died 1793).

Four diamond-shaped *Hatchments* hang in the western part of the nave. These escutcheons, with coats of arms (notice in them the back-to-back squirrels, cracking nuts – the arms of the Samwells) were displayed outside the home of a deceased person for a period of time, before being permanently displayed in the parish church.

They commemorate:-
1. Elizabeth, wife of Sir Wenman Samwell (4th Baronet), who died in 1789. (South wall).

2. Sir Thomas Samwell (1st Baronet), who died in 1693. This hatchment (west wall, south) is probably a later replacement of the original.

3. Sir Thomas Samwell (3rd Baronet) – a bachelor, who died in 1779.

4. Sir Thomas Samwell (2nd Baronet) – who died in 1757.

6. Small rectangular 19th century plaque to Sir William Samwell (died 1627).

7. A plaque by Austin & Seeley of London, with an urn at its summit, to Frances Watson Samwell, widow of Thomas (died 1841).

8. Camilla, sister of Wenman Langham Watson (died 1817); beneath it is a tablet to her, once set in the floor.

Chancel, south wall
9. Sir Thomas Samwell (the 3rd Baronet of that name, who died in 1779).

10. An oval inscription under glass to James Harrington (died 1677), whose mother was the sister of Sir Richard Samwell. He was a friend of King Charles I and of King Charles II and was the author of a book entitled "Oceana". His very distinctive memorial was erected in 1810 by Wenman Langham Watson.

11. A fine plaque with a coat of arms in a cartouche at its apex, to Sir Thomas Samwell (the 2nd Baronet), who died in 1757 and who enlarged and remodelled the Hall. There is a long inscription to him and, beneath, a message to the reader – "Courteous stranger, disturb not his ashes, which are here deposited in expectation of the great and tremendous Day of Judgment, what a man he was".

Heraldic Shields appertaining to Upton and quarters of some are carved on pew ends in the Church and adorn the house (and Spencer Tomb).

The old box pews of Upton Church.

Upton Church prior to the 19th century restoration.

Drawing of Richard Knightley and his lady, interned in Upton Church. Copy from Rev. Serjeantson's "Church of St. Peter, Northampton."

Harrington Memorial tablet in Upton Church.

M. H. HOLDING, A.R.I.B.A.
ARCHITECT.

Corn Exchange.

Northampton May 9 1898

Dear Mr Page

I read with very much interest your letter of appeal which I think is well put together. I shall be pleased to subscribe a guinea in due course. When you had spoken to me on previous occasions about the Choir stalls I am afraid I apparently differed from you with regard to what suitable Choir stalls for the Church would cost + I could not but regret very much the too small amount which you seemed to think would be enough to pay for them. I have had to do with a great many such matters + in Churches of all sizes, + can make money spin out as far I think as anybody but there is a limit as to lowness of cost even when you take into a/c. simplicity, in dealing with oak so that you feel it a case of trying to "make bricks without straw."

Yr. faithfully
M. H. Holding

Walton Page Esq

1898

Mr. Holding's letter to Mr. Page regarding new Choir Stalls

Copy of letter to Mr. Page, Churchwarden, Upton regarding erecting the Holditch Organ in Upton Church 1899.

Dear Mr. Page

I am willing to erect our organ in the West end of Upton Church built by Holditch for the late Lord Chamberlain, Earl Selbourne, containing open diapason and foot (metal) and Tenor c. Viola 8 feet tones, with Vidale, and carved oak case, on appreciation, if the instrument is considered suitable for the building, I will site it to the Churchwarden for sixty pounds (£60). If not satisfactory I will remove New Organ free of cost, and the Churchwardens will not be liable for costs of any kind.

Yours faithfully,

W. Starmer Shaw

April 30th, 1898

The church (with the exception of the tower) was then put in a thorough state of repair, and under the careful supervision of the architect (Mr. M. H. Holding), much interesting work was brought to light. Unfortunately through lack of funds the whole of the intended work could not be carried out. The chancel was left bare, only a temporary deal prayer desk and lectern being provided. At Christmas, 1896 a good Choir of 18 voices was formed, and the provision of Choir stalls has become almost a necessity, as the choristers have to sit on chairs and old borrowed forms, which sadly mar the beauty of the Church. An effort is therefore now being made to supply this want, and also an oak lectern, S. Peter's, Northampton, Young Women's Guild having generously undertaken to give an oak prayer desk. It is also desired, if possible to obtain a small organ, but this will necessitate the building of an organ chamber. As there is no proper vestry it is proposed to build one at the same time, and this is proposed should also be utilised for Sunday School purposes.

Upton Mercury

UPTON CHURCH
THE RECENT RESTORATION

RECEIPTS AND EXPENDITURE TO MAY 17, 1894

===

	RECEIPTS	£.	S.	D.
Oct. 13, 1883	Offertory at Harvest Festival.	3	8	0
June, 1884	Proceeds of Fete in the Grounds of Upton Hall	85	1	2
Feb. 18, 1885	Mr. P.W. Robinson, by Mrs. Turner	3	3	0
Sept. 27, 1885	Offertory at Harvest Festival.	3	6	0
Oct. 3, 1886	Ditto....................................	4	16	0
July, 1889	Mrs. Turner, Proceeds of Hazaar at Upton Hall	100	0	0
	The Right Rev. the Lord Bishop of Peterborough	5	0	0
	The Right Rev. the Bishop of Leicester	4	4	0
	Lord Knightly of Fawsley	5	0	0
	Lady Knightly	2	0	0
	Lady Wantage	5	0	0
	Sir Charles Isham, Bart.	1	0	0
	G. Turner, Esq., the late, Upton Hall	100	0	0
	Mrs. Turner, Upton Hall	50	0	0
	The Chapter of S. Katharine's Hospital, Regent's Park	50	0	0
	The Incorporated Church Building Society	20	0	0
	The Northamptonshire Ditto	10	0	0
	The Rev. E.N. Tom, Rector.	55	0	0
	The Rev. J.H. Glover	10	10	0
	Mrs. Whitworth, the late	10	0	0
	W. Wright Esq.	10	0	0
	Mr. T.G. Turner	13	0	0
	Mrs. T.G. Turner	1	1	0
	Mr. C. Turner	10	0	0
	Mr. W. Jeffery	10	0	0
	Mr. C. E. Thorpe	10	0	0
	Miss Crow	5	0	0
	Richard Phipps, Esq.	5	0	0
	Watts-Manning, Esq.	5	0	0
	Mr. T. Manning	5	0	0
	Mr. J. Wade	5	0	0
	A. Friend	5	0	0
	Anonymous – A Thank-offering	5	0	0
	Mrs. Facer, the late	4	0	0
	R. Lee Bevan, Esq.	3	3	0
	R. S. Boddington, Esq.	3	3	0
	Mr. M.H. Holding	3	3	0
	W. Butlin, Esq.	3	0	0
	Mr. Garner, Harpole	3	0	0
	Mr. Spokes, Upton	3	0	0
	The Rev. Canon Birch	2	0	0
	Mrs. Thornton, Kingsthorpe Hall	2	0	0
	Miss Eleanor Thornton, Ditto	2	0	0
	Dr. Greene	2	2	0
	Dr. Faulkner	2	2	0
	J. Haviland, Esq.	2	2	0
	J. Barry, Esq.	2	2	0
	Mr. T. Osborn	2	2	0
	Mrs. Osborn	1	1	0
	Mrs. Higgins	2	2	0
	Mrs. Dunkley, Kislingbury	2	2	0
	Mr. W. Shepherd	2	2	0
	Mrs. Jones	2	2	0
	Mr. J. R. Buxton	2	0	0
	The Rev. Canon Smith	1	1	0
	F. H. Thornton, Esq.	1	0	0
	The Rev. J. Phillips	1	1	0
	Mrs. Phillips	0	10	6
	The Rev. A. A. Longhurst, the late	1	0	0
	H. P. Gates, Esq., the late	1	0	0
	Messrs. Mobbs & Smith	1	1	0
	Mr. Joseph Hanson	1	0	0
	Mr. J. Lovell, Dodford	1	0	0
	A Friend	1	0	0
	Miss Smith, formerly of Upton	1	0	0
	Mr. W. Faulkner, Upton	1	0	0
	Mr. F. Stimpson	1	0	0
	Mr. Croxton Smith	1	1	0
	Mr. Tucker	1	0	0
	The Rev. W. T. Fry	1	1	0
	The Rev. C. R. Barker	1	1	0
	Mr. Barriball	1	1	0
	Mr. Davies, S. Peter's	1	6	0
	The Rev. Canon Bury	1	0	0
	The Rev. R. D. L. Clarke	1	1	0
	The Rev. J. B. Wickes	1	1	0
	The Rev. T. S. Hichens	1	1	0
	The Rev. E. L. Tuson	1	1	0
	Mrs. Griffin	1	0	0
	Mr. G. Norman	1	1	0
	The Rev. L. R. Loyd	1	1	0
	Mrs. Howes	0	10	0
	Mr. Tomes	0	10	6
	Mr. E. K. Elliott, Towcester	0	5	0
	Mrs. Smith, Upton	0	5	0
	Mrs. Harris, Ditto	0	5	0
	Mr. W. Bray, Ditto	0	2	0
	Mrs. W. Bray, Ditto	0	2	0
	Mrs. Gausden, Ditto	0	2	0
	Mrs. Burrows, Ditto	0	2	0
	Mrs. Anderson	0	2	0
	Anonymous	0	1	0
	The Rector, Fees	3	7	10
	Box in Church	2	7	0
Mar. 16, 1893	Offertories at Re-opening	75	19	0
Mar. 19, 1893	Ditto	7	14	0
1890	Ditto, Harvest Festival	4	8	0
1891	Ditto ditto	3	11	9
1893	Ditto ditto	5	8	2
	Interest at Bank	33	8	9
	Deficit	201	5	1
		£1034	4	9

62

EXPENDITURE

Date	Item	£	S.	D.
Sept. 1889	Advertising Harvest Festivals to this date	0	14	6
Oct. 1891	Stanton, Printing 150 Circular Appeals	0	9	6
Jan. 1892	Northampton Herald, Advertising	0	7	0
	Northampton Mercury, Ditto	0	4	0
	B. W. Gates, Esq, for Faculty	2	4	6
Sept. 1892	Stanton, Printing 2nd Appeal and list	0	9	6
Mar. 16, 1893	Clerk. day of Re-Opening	0	5	0
May, 1893	Northampton Herald, Advertising Reopening	0	15	3
	Northampton Mercury, Ditto	0	14	9
Oct. 1893	Stanton, Printing Notices of Reopening	0	8	6
Aug. 30, 1892	Mr. J. T. Wingrove, Builder	300	0	0
Oct. 28, 1892	Ditto Ditto	150	0	0
Feb. 1, 1893	Ditto Ditto	250	0	0
Mar. 21, 1893	Ditto Ditto	200	0	0
Dec. 22, 1893	Ditto, Balance of Account	82	16	9
Feb. 17, 1893	Mr. M. H. Holding, Architect, on Account	30	0	0
Apr. 4, 1893	Mr. Shoosmith, Hire of Chairs	0	10	0
July 13, 1893	Mr. W. Wright, Far Cotton, for Hassocks, & c	5	18	0
Jan. 1894	Advertising Harvest Festival, 1893	0	4	6
	Stamps for sending Notices of Re-opening	0	9	9
	Bank Charges to this date	7	13	3
		£1034	4	9

May 17, 1894 examined with Vouchers and found correct,

J. SPOKES, Churchwarden.

The above deficit – £201.5s.1d. – is the amount now due at the bank, and there is yet due to the Architect, £32.18s.3d., making £234.3s.4d.: towards which the Rector has promised £25 this year. This will leave £209.3s.4d. still to raise, and the Bank interest will soon add to it.

The debt, however, will be substantially reduced, no doubt, by the Sale of Work at Upton Hall, which Mrs. Turner is kindly providing for next Thursday, May 24th. But much will, necessarily, remain to be raised, and the Rector will gratefully receive further help towards defraying it.

GIFTS TO THE CHURCH

Mrs. Turner, Vestry Curtains, Miss Druffill, The Altar Vases, Mrs. Tom, Alms' Dish, S. Peters's Young Women's Guild, Bible and Prayer Book.

FURTHER NEEDS

which it is hoped, will be supplied before very long:- a new Font, new Prayer Desk, new Lectern, Choir Stalls, New Doors for north door of Nave, and southe door of Chancel.

The Rector records his deep thankfulness to almighty God that the Restoration has been so nearly completed and also his gratitude to all who have kindly helped in the work.

E. N. TOM

S. Peter's Rectory, Northampton,
May 17, 1894.

It is also desired if possible to obtain a small organ, but this will necessitate the building of an organ chamber. As there is no proper vestry it is proposed to build this at the same time and being part of the same structure it would entail but little additional expense.

The whole of the proposed work is estimated to cost about £350.

The congregation consists almost entirely of working people (cottagers and the wives and children of the attendants at Berry Wood Asylum which is in the parish of Upton) and it is as much as they can do to maintain the services in their present state of efficiency. We are therefore compelled to appeal to the generosity of friends outside our parish, and we venture to earnestly solicit your assistance. Subscriptions, however small would be most gratefully received, and duly acknowledged. Cheques can be most payable to the "Upton Choir Stalls Fund," (Capital and Counties Bank)

We are yours faithfully

E. N. TOM, S. Peter's Rectory, Northampton, Rector.
W. T. BATTEN, Upton Lawn.
WALTON PAGE, Park House, Upton

Obituary, 1913

The Rev. E. N. Tom

In Northampton, ordained in 1858, he came to Northampton as curate of Kingsthorpe in 1860, and had since remained in the town making a large number of friends and no enemies. In 1873 he was appointed rector of St. Peters, with Upton, and for 32 years laboured in these parishes, beloved by all for his devotion to duty and kindly charitable actions. In him the poor had a friend, the sick and suffering a consoler, and many a parishioner in difficulties has had cause to bless the valuable advice given in return for confidence placed in the rector. Eight years ago failing sight and impaired health made it necessary for Mr. Tom to relinquish his rectorate, and he retired in 1905 with the sympathy and affection of the parishioners.

Other fine woodwork which adorns the church was made by Messrs Jones & Willis of Great Russell Street, London in 1907-8. This includes the *pulpit,* with its splendidly carved panels of crocketted ogee arches framing linenfold designs, the arcaded Communion rails, the altar and the fine reredos, where we see the Archangels Michael (with dragon), and Gabriel (with scroll upon which is "Ave Maria"), carvings of wheat and a grape-vine (for the Blessed Sacrament) and a central recess with diaper-work.

1980. The organ was removed from Upton Church, completely overhauled and is now at St. Benedict Hunsbury Hill and with its Oak Choir Pews will return to St. Michael's whenever it reopens. There is a plaster relief *carving of St. Michael* (c. 1910), with his flaming sword and surrounded by angels. In 1907-8 the western *vestry screen* was made by Jones & Willis, who also produced the woodcarving which lines the *north door.*

Rev. Serjeantson, M.A., FSA, 1822-1891.

His spare time was filled, not only by historical studies, but also by the pursuit of natural history. Another enthusiast recalled how he and Serjeantson went one summer's Sunday afternoon towards Peterborough. They became so absorbed in botanizing that they missed the train back to Northampton. Serjeantson was very upset to realise that he could not now return in time for evensong. They both laughed and decided to botanize on.

Robert Serjeantson graduated from Keble College, Oxford. He was rector of St Peter's from 1906 to 1916. He died in that year from pneumonia, said to be owing to overwork. A photograph shows a dark-haired man with a generous look and a full black beard. A very few among us can still remember him. He was buried in his family's church at Acton Burnall, Salop, but he was entitled as rector to a memorial in St. Peter's sanctuary. The large wall brass was probably of his own design and certainly shows his absorption in medieval tradition including heraldry. The cross on three steps with chalice and host at its foot denotes him a priest. The inscription in Latin mentions that he was a fellow of the Society of Antiquaries of London. He was outstanding among our rectors.

D.G.S.

(David Sargant) Historian, St. Peter's Church, Northampton.

Church Mass (or Scratch Dials)

Mass Dials, or Scratch Dials are to be found on, or outside, many of the old churches in our own area and are believed to date from the 8th Century A.D.

Little is known about them, only that they were there for timing Mass (Latin). A metal peg (Gnomon) was inserted in the centre hole.

Sandstone Churches were ideal for "Scratching" whereas others built of hard stone had dials painted on. The one at Upton is in the South Porch, and is like so many on Church buildings which have been removed as changes and additions to the buildings were made over the Centuries and replaced elsewhere.

The Monastic services began at Midnight with Matins, Mass at 3 am and 6 am and so on through the day. All those forms of services ended at the Reformation. The traditional Church clock began to appear in the 15th Century and, often faulty, were checked by the more regular timepiece the Sundial, which became popular in the 18th Century. It was said that a Mass dial could be read in all but the dullest weather whereas we tend to associate them only with the Sun. After reading the dial the priest would toll the bell for worship. Also the timing bell was used for workers in the fields or tolled for a death in the village.

Many years ago at Upper Harlestone I was surprised to find at the old Laundry Stone buildings a Mass Dial about 4ft from ground level next to the old Dovecote, a sure sign of a Monastic order.

There are plenty of Sundials to be found on Church Walls usually high up on the Towers. Over the south porch at Upton one can see on the datestone where the metal plaque, with its central metal rod could have been. These Church sundials are attributed to the 18th Century.

Bells of St. Michael's Church, Upton

In 1700 there were three bells in the belfry of St. Michael's, Upton. The first and second were inscribed "R.A. 1614", and were cast by Robert Atton of Buckingham. In 1975 there were only two, described as follows: No 1. Diameter 30½ in, with inscription. "Sancta Maria O[ra] P[ro nobis]". This has a shield showing initials "T. N." (Thomas Newcombe of Leicester). No. 2, Priest's Bell, no inscription. The Church clock, which can only be read from the front of the Hall, is by Smiths of Derby, with a pin wheel escapement. This drives gearing level with the floor above the bells, and strikes the hour on the large bell when the weights for the clock are wound up to something like 40 feet high in the Tower. They are about seven days falling, so the Sexton would only need to climb up the dusty narrow stone steps every Saturday morning. The death-knell using the old tenor bell in the villages around was three tolls for a man, two for a woman and one for a child, and for the funeral the tenor bell would be muffled.

At each end of the Victorian Riga, oak pews are elaborate carvings of the many Samwells' Coats of Arms.

The oak clergy stalls placed in St. Michael's by the Young Women's Guild of St. Peter's, Northampton and St. Michael's, Upton. The two churches were annexed for over 250 years.

Part Five – Berrywood

Introduction to Berrywood Hospital

This book is recalling the early years of this Mental Hospital from 1870 to 1948.

Some of the story of old Berrywood is observed with interviews with retired male and female nurses who came from Ireland, Wales etc., to train there. Many married and lived either in the hospital or in the village of Duston. Their stories tell of caring for and devotion to the patients, long hours and little time off, with long night duties looking after large numbers of people. A large number of men found employment in skilled trades at the hospital such as plumbers, decorators, carpenters, butchers, farm workers, kitchen gardeners etc. It was estimated that for some 1,400 patients a similar amount of men and women directly or indirectly were employed to do the work. Great changes eventually came about, beginning with the Health Authority in 1948, and continuing through the 50's, 60's and 70's. It resulted in the improving health of all the patients and their freedom from the institutional atmosphere. The walls came down, doors were unlocked and new skills were taught. Mr. Burrell, secretary and finance officer to the hospital, Mr. Kempster, chief male nurse, (both now retired) were instrumental in these great changes, with many others. So much so that eventually the hospital was the envy of British Mental Hospitals, and Mr. Burrell was to travel in an advisory capacity to institutions all over the country. By then it was St. Crispin's Hospital. Now almost all the occupants have gone, and soon will be part of the Western housing for expanding Northampton, although still part of the Parish of Upton.

The authorities attention was drawn to 180 acres of freehold land at Upton for sale with a good road through the estate ringed by an iron fence and pleasant areas of woods and a good supply of water. This was Berrywood Farm, of 190 acres, for centuries part of the Upton 2,000 acre estate put up for sale owing to the insolvency of the estate after the death of the last member of the Samwell family. With no direct heir, distant relatives claimed the property. For some 40 years, the whole of the buildings, the Hall and Farm property fell into disrepair. The Church was closed and the trustees first of all sold Berrywood Farm.

By August 1970 agreement was reached to purchase Berrywood with the Commissioners in Lunacy, after inspecting the site in November 1970. The Infirmary accounts show a bill for 5/- for their cab visit to the site with 6d for the Cab driver. The purchase of the property was authorised by parliament and the final deed of conveyance of the property for the County was signed in August 1871. The land £14,350 – the timber on the site £2,120.

The Committees were responsible for the building of the Asylum for an agreed total of 400 pauper Lunatics, and upon the advice of the Commissioners of Lunacy, numerous designs were sent to two leading Architects, Professor T. Donaldson and Mr. T. H. Wyatt who favoured plans submitted by Mr. Griffiths, County Surveyor of Staffordshire, chiefly on account of their architectural character in keeping with the purposes for which the buildings were intended. In January 1872, the final plans were approved. After tenders were invited, the building contract was awarded to Messrs Smith Bros of Northampton. As the buildings were near completion, the post of Medical Superintendent was advertised offering a salary of £500 a year with gas, water, rates and taxes paid.

The roads and approaches to the asylum are also in a very rough and unfinished state.

The building operations have been prolonged much beyond the time specified in the contract, and the estimate has been considerably exceeded. There are now 106 workmen employed about the place, and there does not appear to be any prospect of the original buildings, together with the farm buildings and cottages.

At dinner in the hall we saw men and 127 women, and about this number have all their meals here together. The conduct of all was orderly, and the dinner, consisting of boiled pork, bread and potatoes, with beer, seems generally liked. The diet is similar to that adopted in the Middlesex and Metropolitan Asylums, consisting of tea or cocoa and bread and butter for breakfast; bread and cheese and beer, or bread and butter and tea, for supper, for the men; and bread and butter and tea for the women. Solid meat for dinner, with vegetables and bread, is given on four days of the week, and meat pie on one. Fish or Irish stew, or soup with vegetables or rice, on one day, and Irish stew with bread, on one day. Beer is allowed daily.

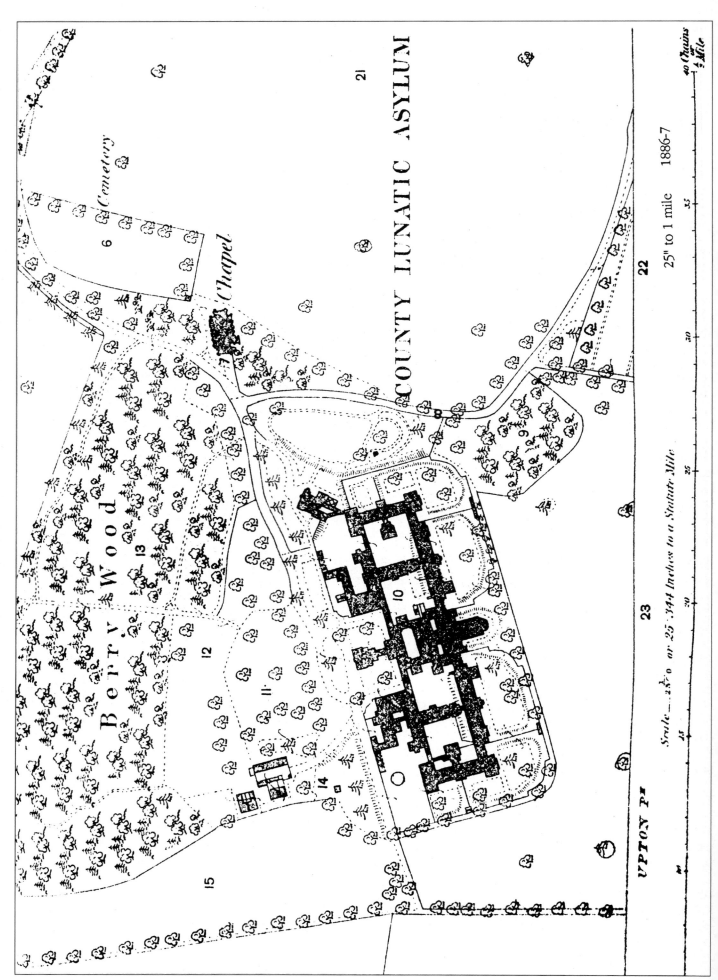

COUNTY LUNATIC ASYLUM

Berry Wood

Cemetery

Chapel

25" to 1 mile   1886-7

Scale — 2520 or 25·344 Inches to a Statute Mile.

40 Chains
½ Mile

UPTON P⁸

Map reproduced from "Ordnance Survey Mapping" as dated by permission.

68

The arrangements with regard to the attendants are somewhat exceptional. It is the rule that the male wards should be cleared of all whom it is possible to send out of doors, at quarter to seven in the morning, and that the wards should not be reoccupied till half past Six in the morning. The men so going out are employed on the land or at different trades and occupations, under the supervision of Labourers and Artisans, who however have received a certain amount of training as attendants of the insane. Those who remain in the wards are looked after by women, who receive a gratuity of £2 a year in addition to their ordinary wages.

The staff consists, on the male side, of a Male Inspector, Head Female Attendant, two first-class Female Attendants, three second-class Females, and 16 Farm Labourers. On the female side, of a Head Female Attendant, five first-class and nine second-class Attendants.

Attendants – The Head Female Attendant is over both divisions. There are also two night attendants for the men and three for the women. One in each division remains continuously in the rooms respectively devoted to the use of epileptic and suicidal patients, whilst the others make their rounds once every hour.

The wages are as Follows:- Male Inspector, £50 per annum; Housekeeper, £45; Head Female Attendant, £40, First-class Labourer, £30 to £40; Second-class, £25 to £35; First-class Female, £18 to £30; Second-class, £15 to £25.

The Night Attendants are in the position of First-Class Attendants. Board of course is also given in all cases, as well as a uniform. Prayers are read every morning and evening by the Chaplain in the hall, when 80 men and 100 women are present, and the same number attend Divine Service twice on Sunday.

The number of patients usefully employed daily is among the males 190, more than a hundred of whom are employed in farmwork; and among the females 160, in sewing, laundry, and housework.

Twice a week the working patients are allowed a half holiday, and, occasionally, from 40 to 50 of each sex are taken out for walks. A weekly dance is given, which is attended by a considerable number, sometimes as many as 140 to 150 of both sexes.

We saw seven men at work in the tailor's and ten in the shoemaker's shop, and the returns give 102 as the total numbers employed, of whom 36 work in the garden; of the women, 124 are employed, 11 of them helping in the laundry, and 36 doing needlework.

Northampton County Hospital

How it was established, a report of its opening in 1876 and subsequent reports

The land was bought and the Asylum was erected and furnished at a cost of £162,176 14s 7d., of which the sum of £149,600 was borrowed, and of this sum £63,280 has already been paid.

The Asylum may now be regarded as completed, and the offices and wards provided with fittings and furniture. The Contractors have left the building in the hands of the county.

Seven cottages have been built for the artizans employed in the Asylum.

The farm buildings with a cottage for the bailiff, are completed, and are in the process of being occupied. Stables have also been built.

Fire hydrants, at the suggestion of the Commissioners in Lunacy, have been fixed throughout the building.

The kitchen apparatus and engineering work generally, as well as the gas works and sewage arrangements, are in a satisfactory condition.

The Asylum was opened on the 30th June 1876, and on that day, and during the following week, 61 males and 54 females were transferred here from the Northampton General Lunatic Hospital.

The Asylum is situated at Berry Wood, about 2½ miles from Northampton. The site, consisting of 200 acres, is elevated, with cheerful and extensive views, and the land is admirably adapted for sewage irrigation.

The building is arranged for the reception of 270 patients of each sex, with offices of a sufficient size for a still larger number, and the general arrangements appear to have been carefully studied by the architect. It is of red and white brick, and the work seems to have been well and substantially executed. The interior is plastered throughout, the woodwork is excellent.

1876

On the 30th June, 1876, H. P. Markham, Esq., having been appointed Clerk to the Visitors; Dr. Millson, Medical Superintendent; Dr. Bowes, Assistant Medical Officer; and Mr. F. A. Robinson, Clerk of the Asylum. On the 31st of December, 1877, it contained 510 patients, 291 being chargeable to the County of Northampton, and 85 to the Boroughs of Northampton and Peterborough. The remainder were admitted from the County of Essex, the Borough of Birmingham, and the Three Counties (Bedford, Hereford, and Huntingdon).

The Rate of Maintenance charged to the Northamptonshire Unions was 11/- per head per week; to the Boroughs of Northampton and Peterborough 13/-; and to other Counties and Boroughs 14/-.

All the floors are of pitch pine and well laid, and the lighting of the day rooms, corridors, and dormitories is good. The Superintendent's house is at the North-East angle, communicating by a short corridor with the male division. In the centre are the Committee-room, Clerk's and Superintendent's offices, the kitchen and Servant's hall, and the other usual departmental offices. The dining and recreation hall is in the centre to the south. The blocks for patients are the same on either side, and consist of six wards in each division. Those for males are completed, but only two wards and a dormitory are at present occupied on the female side. Temporarily a certain number of women are in some of the wards in the male division. Thus a few occupy the wards, 8 and 9 by day, whilst the dormitory No 12 is specially set apart for the night use of the female suicidal and epileptic patients. The 1st and 2nd floors however in the further female block are nearly completed, and may shortly be occupied. Beside the County and Borough patients which may thus be accommodated, there will remain a considerable amount of space, which may be available for out County patients.

The chapel is in a very unfinished state, and little progress has been made in the levelling and formation of the airing courts. The want of them is said to be not much felt, as the patients are sent out for walks beyond the grounds. At the same time we think that no time should be lost in turfing and planting them, and getting them generally in proper order.

1878

Of the 190 acres, comprising the whole estate, about 70 are now in possession, and are being cultivated by the attendants and patients.

The casualties have not been very numerous; four were important and call for notice. A patient, S. R., sustained a fracture of the fibula from a kick by another patient; L. C., a fracture of left arm in struggling with another patient; J. W., a fracture of the right thigh in falling down; and S. H., a fracture of right arm, also in falling down.

Five patients at different periods managed to effect their escape from the Asylum, and not having been retaken within the fourteen days, were discharged. Three of the patients belonged to the Liberty of Peterborough, one to the County of Essex, and one to the Borough of Northampton.

There are 31 epileptic females and 47 epileptic males who are under constant supervision at night, and to ensure the watchfulness of the attendant in charge of each epileptic dormitory, the Tell-tale-clock is required to be registered every ten minutes.

About a hundred and sixty patients of each sex take their meals in the dining hall, and the arrangement for cutting up and keeping hot of the food in the kitchen works satisfactorily.

The laundries, workshops, dressing and sewing-rooms are equal to the requirements of the building, and they are efficiently managed by the several officers in charge of them.

Since the sinking of the second well, there has been an adequate supply of water, but I am afraid that before long an additional set of well pumps will have to be procured, as those now in use are barely sufficient to keep the tower-tank supplied with water.

The hydrants for extinguishing fire that have recently been put up, are in good working order, and the attendants are being trained in the management of them. I am not, however, quite satisfied that there would be a sufficient supply of water should such a misfortune as a fire take place.

Northampton County Lunatic Asylum was the outcome of an act of Parliament in 1888 requiring all local authorities to build an Asylum for pauper lunatics from money raised from rate. At that time consideration was being given for establishing a ward at the General Infirmary Hospital for lunacy patients although a sum of £552 was raised by donations.

The old Northampton Lunatic Asylum later called St. Andrews was opened in 1838, patients paying their own accommodation, some able to pay the entire cost, others partly meeting the cost of their Maintenance there.

Pauper lunatics were later admitted. After some eighteen years an agreement was reached between the Justices of the peace and the Directors of the Hospital whereby the sum of 27/- per week per head was paid for their lodging.

The Government was not happy with this agreement and pressed for a Pauper Asylum to be built as soon as possible and by 1870 the Commissioners in Lunacy condemned the agreement of paid mental patients and paupers at Northampton Lunatic Asylum where the paid would have access to the best wards there.

1880

Much was done this year to improve the Estate by planting trees and shrubs and putting up iron fencing. The Airing Courts were also improved.

An additional set of Pumps were placed in the Well and another Engine was fitted up in the Engine-room.

A large barn and implement Shed were added to the Farm Buildings. A slight and very inexpensive alteration was made in the General Store-Room whereby Stores could more conveniently be delivered to the Kitchen.

The year 1880 closed with 557 patients in the Asylum, being 17 in excess of the number which the Building was originally planned for, and 44 above the number for the year before. Of the increase, upwards of half were chargeable to Northamptonshire.

An Addition was made to the Medical Superintendent's house, and two Cottages were built for Farm Servants.

In the Asylum 10 additional beds were obtained on the male side by converting a Lavatory into a Dormitory and building a new Lavatory in a more suitable place than the old one. On the female side the Sewing-room was made into a 10-bedded Dormitory.

On the first of January the Rate of Maintenance was reduced to 10/-, and at the same time the Diet-scale was revised and improved.

1881

Mr. Turner, a wealthy boot and shoe manufacturer purchased in 1881 the rest of the estate and devoted his life in restoring the Hall, Church and Farm buildings.

The Report for 1881 shows a still further increase in the number of inmates of the Asylum. The Northamptonshire cases had risen to 448, and the total reached 590. This entailed a little overcrowding in some of the wards, and to do away with this two courses only were open to the Visitors:-

    1st.   To discharge a certain number of the paying cases, or
    2nd.   To enlarge the Asylum.

In this year, the means for prevention of Fire and for the safety of the patients in the event of fire breaking out, occupied the attention of the visitors. A large Manual Fire Engine, a Fire Escape, a number of small corridor Engines, and a good supply of Fire Buckets were provided. The Fire Brigade is regularly drilled and occasional alarms are sounded. The Fire Engine can be brought into use in three minutes and the indoor appliances in two minutes or less.

In addition to some minor alterations in the main Building, Cottages for the Head Attendant and Engineer were built close to the Asylum.

The Visitors, after an exhaustive discussion, now decided to increase the accommodation by adding Dayroom and Dormitory space for 160 patients. This course was not embarked on without carefully weighing all the circumstances; but the points which seemed to justify the steps were:-

1st. That the additions would enable the general plan and arrangements to be greatly improved. For instance the Dormitories for Epileptics were on the third stories of the old Building, and in the new Blocks they would be placed on the ground floor. Then there were no proper means for watching the Suicidal cases by night, and special Dormitories would be set apart for this purpose.

1884

On the 31st December, 1884, the numbers had risen to 573. Of these, 491 were Home cases, 36 were Private Patients, and 146 were from other Counties.

There was no direct communication between the second stories of Blocks No. 1 and No. 2, and the one floor could only be reached from the other by a very roundabout way. Fireproof passages were constructed on the first floor levels. These were built on arches, and the Arcade on the ground level afforded a much-wanted shelter from sun or rain for those patients using the South Airing Courts.

The main Chimney, which had shown signs of weakness, was this year pulled down and rebuilt. This course was recommended by an Expert, consulted by the visitors.

The Farm Buildings received an important addition in the shape of a Dutch Barn and Silo, and four Cottages for married Attendants were built on the Estate.

The most important thing to mention in connection with the year 1886 was the erection of a detached Hospital for the treatment of infectious diseases. It possesses ample room for 14 Fever cases, and, when not wanted for its special purpose, forms a very pleasant residence for about 26 harmless cases. The Hospital cost £2,700.

Also during this year the Visitors carefully went into the question of providing a separate Block for the treatment of Idiot children, and a Sub-committee, consisting of the Duke of Grafton, Colonel Rawlins, Edward Grant, Esq, and Pickering Phipps, Esq., visited the Idiot Asylums at Lancaster, Earlswood, and Colchester, and subsequently reported on the question generally. The Sub-committee recommended that a Block for 48 or 50 children should be erected near the West corner of the Asylum, and connected with the main Building by a fireproof Corridor. Plans embodying the above were prepared by the Medical Superintendent and forwarded to the Commissioners in Lunacy.

The open-door system of Asylum management was more fully developed than it had hitherto been at Berry Wood, and it was reported that 500 patients were not under lock and key during the greater part of the day.

This was the Jubilee year of Her Majesty's reign, and the event was celebrated in a suitable manner by the entire staff and 450 of the patients.

The number had risen to 704, and once more the Rate of Maintenance was reduced. This time to 7/6 a week, being upwards of a shilling lower than the average of English Asylums.

1887. Although 839 suicidal Cases have been under treatment it may be noted that no Suicide has yet occurred in this Asylum. (During the year ending 31st December, 1887, there were 123 Suicides in the English Public Asylums).

Thirty-six Lunatic Criminals have been sent to the Asylum under warrant of the Secretary of State for the Home Department. The visitors would leave on record their opinion that some effective means should be given to the visitors to refuse to receive such cases.

The Asylum Farm has been carried on with great advantage to the Asylum. A certain quantity of land must be attached to every Asylum, and outdoor exercise is beneficial to the patients. It may indeed be said that independently of the great service rendered by the Farm towards the management and treatment of the patients, the Asylum has to farm from necessity as well as from choice.

It is worthy of note that the Clerk to the visitors, the Medical Superintendent, the Clerk of the Asylum, the Head Attendant, the Head Nurse, the Housekeeper, and the Farm Bailiff have all had upwards of ten year's service in the Asylum. The Assistant Medical Officer and the Storekeeper have had upwards of five year's service. Among the Attendants, Nurses, Artisans, and Domestics there are seventeen who have been ten years in the Asylum and twenty who have been five years.

Early in the year there was an outbreak of dysenteric diarrhoea in the Asylum, and the Committee, in accordance with the suggestions of the Commissioners in Lunacy, called in Mr. Bohn; who, as an expert, reported upon the drainage and ventilation of the Asylum.

The Committee purchased from Mr. S. Garner, three fields to the west of the Asylum, containing about 53 acres of land for the sum of £3,020.

The question of the rating of the Asylum was considered this year and a Committee was appointed to meet the Assessment Committee; and it was agreed between the two Committees that the assessment should be reduced from £3,429 to £2,699.

1888

In 1888 the Block for idiot children, which cost £3,500, was opened, and a new departure was seen in the objects of the Asylum, namely, the training and care of this unfortunate class. So far as the experiment has been tried at Berry Wood, it must be pronounced a complete success.

The Visitors on their inspections of the Asylum, often felt that the system of dining patients in a common hall had numerous drawbacks and scarcely any compensatory advantages. At the same time it was evident that the meals could not be properly served in the ordinary Day-rooms. It was therefore decided to extend the small Dining-rooms already attached to the infirmary and Acute Wards, and build new ones for the other wards. These have been finished and each of the eleven wards has now its own proper dining-room. The second floor of these new Blocks to the South is devoted to Attendant's-rooms and to a few single-bedded rooms for patients. There is also space in the Gallery leading to these rooms for a considerable number of beds, but it is intended not to use this space unless it were necessary to transfer the patients from the infectious Hospital owing to outbreak of infectious disease.

1889

On the 30th March, 1889, the total number of patients was 662, showing a decrease of 42 in the numbers resident on the last day of 1887; this decrease being owing to the removal of the patients chargeable to the Counties of Essex and Leicester.

The entire capacity of the Asylum, including Children's Block and infectious Hospital, may be recorded at 850 beds. It would seem that additions lately made to other County Asylums show an average cost of about £90 a bed. At Berry Wood the cost has been considerably under £50, and this includes Dining-rooms, Visiting room, and other minor additions.

As already stated these additions have, without exception, been built with the profits accruing from the out-county and private patients; and not only this but the Building has been kept in repair from the same source, no call having ever been made on the County Rate for materials or for artisan's wages.

Since the opening of the Asylum, 2,651 patients have been admitted; 1,204 have been discharged; and 785 have died. The Visitors have always encouraged of course under proper safeguards, the discharge of harmless chronic cases to their own homes, and 99 such are included in the number of discharges above-mentioned. Only 19 of these have been sent back to the Asylum, and, although some have died, a great many are enjoying their liberty, and a considerable saving to the rates has resulted from the course pursued.

1892

A sitting-room for male attendants was built in 1892 at a cost of £150. New entrance gates were also provided at a cost of £78.

A new steam fire engine, costing £415, was also purchased from Messrs. Shand, Mason & CO.; and a house for the same was erected at a cost of £150.

Two new cottages were built on the estate at a cost of £540.

Early this year various headings were made in the old well in order to increase the water supply, and it was ultimately decided to construct a new well. Before this was done however, the Committee resolved to employ Mr. Mullens, the water finder, to report on the probable position of water under the estate. Mr. Mullens accordingly attended at the Asylum one day in April, "went over a great part of the estate marking those parts where he was of opinion water could be obtained. His opinion was founded on the turning of a twig in his hands. He went round the ground adjoining the new cottages being built on the Nobottle Road but was satisfied no water could be obtained there.

The Committee then decided to sink a new well in the position which Mr. Bohn might consider most favourable for the purpose. Tenders were obtained and that of Mr. Wingrove for carrying out the work being the lowest was accepted.

1893

Operations were accordingly commenced forthwith and continued until March, 1893 when it was reported that a depth of 259 feet below the level of the ground plan of the Asylum had been reached and that there was no sign of water.

Mr. Beeby Thompson was consulted and he reported on the 18th April that in his opinion the boring should be continued for another 50 feet, when he thought the water-bearing bed of Marlstone or Middle Lias would be reached.

The following month Mr. Beeby Thompson made another report very much to the same effect.

In June, Mr. Beeby Thompson reported that the hard rock in the well had been pierced, and stiff blue clay reached; and that he considered the Committee might safely rely on a yield of 100,000 gallons a day.

The tender of Messrs. Batchelor for sinking a new well by the boring with a larger pump and powerful windmill for the sum of £2,849, was then accepted.

The work was accordingly proceeded with and the well was sunk and headings made and the water proved abundant. In October, 1894, it was reported that the well produced 30,000 gallons of water a day, and a little later this increased to 40,000 gallons a day.

The new well was ultimately completed, with pumps, windmill and mains. The total sum paid to Mr. Batchelor, being £4,452 8s 7d, for the work; and the sum of £791 11 s 7d. was paid to Mr. Wingrove for sinking the earlier well, which proved a failure.

A dormitory for epileptic and suicidal patients was erected the same year, at a cost of £500.

The Telegraph station at Duston was established in 1886 on a guarantee given by the Committee of this Asylum.

1894

This was renewed in July, 1894, for a further term of seven years at a yearly rent of £18, less the sum received in payment for telegrams sent from Duston.

Letter to the Editor

The Divining Rod

1894. To the Editor of the *Northampton Mercury*

Sir, Some time ago the Berry Wood Asylum Committee paid a man five guineas and his expenses for, as they thought, finding water for them. He indicated a spot where he told them there was plenty of water at 80ft deep. I have today received an anonymous letter from "a large ratepayer," who gives me the following information. Of course it may be all wrong, and he may be simply playing a practical joke upon my turn. I am credulous, and believe what he says. He says that the well was made where the divining rod indicated water has been sunk to 280ft, and that there is no water excepting six or seven gallons when the men get there to work in the morning. He says £3,200 has been spent, in addition to the five guineas and expenses paid to the divining rod man in this attempt to find water. He also says he hears that an adjoining field of 22 acres could have been purchased, and that on this field there is a spring yielding 48,000 gallons every 24 hours. I understand him to say that since the magic man was there two wells have been sunk, one twenty yards from the other. He says, "I know it is well to be wise after the event, but before the last contractor commenced the committee had the experience of the first attempt." Surely all this is enough to open the eyes of the people who believe in the divining rod! I am, yours, truly,

THOS JUDGE
Brackley, April 8, 1894.

1897

The Jubilee, on the 22nd June, 1897, was celebrated at the Asylum by a general holiday, an extra dinner to patients and staff, outdoor sports in the afternoon, dances in the evening, bonfire, and dance for the staff on the following day.

The kitchen was entirely remodelled and greatly enlarged at a cost of about £1,500, new ranges and other appliances being obtained at a cost of £527 10s 0d.

Miss McDonald was appointed Housekeeper, and the following year Head Nurse.

1900

On the enlargements of the boundary of the Borough of Northampton in 1900, forty-one pauper patients who had become chargeable to the Northampton and Hardingstone Unions, were transferred to and became chargeable to the Borough of Northampton.

This year a Stevenson's Screen, with certified maximum and minimum thermometers, was provided, in order that records of temperature, as well as of rainfall should be taken.

1901

At the January meeting held in 1901, the Chairman, Mr. W. Hirst Simpson, in feeling terms referred to the lamented demise of our late Gracious Sovereign Queen Victoria and moved the following resolution, which was carried unanimously:-

That a minute be made of the profound feelings of the Committee, that in the death of Her Majesty a great national loss has been sustained by the Country; and that the Committee were moved by deep and sincere emotion of humble sympathy with His Majesty the King and all the members of His Royal House."

1903

The late Mr. William Walter Slye, of Thorndale House, West Haddon, Northamptonshire, who died on the 16th November, 1903, by his Will bequeathed "To the Treasurer or Treasurers, for the time being, of the Lunatic Asylum at Berry Wood, Northampton. One Thousand Pounds, to be applied to and for the benefit and for the purposes of the said Asylum." This bequest was received in June the following year. An organ was then purchased for the chapel at a cost of £350, and the remainder of the money was invested in the purchase of thirteen Debentures of the Northampton Electric Light and Power Company Limited.

1904

Early in the year 1904 a new oil engine of 16-horse power was ordered for pumping water from the well, at cost of £194 10s 0d.

Mr. H. Mansfield, in June, moved and it was resolved that a small infectious Hospital to be erected to accommodate eight patients, at an estimated cost of £2,000. The plans for this were considered by the Committee at the January meeting the following year, and duly approved by the Commissioners.

1905

The Committee, at the April meeting in 1905, passed a vote of condolence with the widow and family of the late Mr. Westley, a member of the Committee.

During the year the plans for the new Laundry were considered, and were afterwards approved by the Commissioners. At the November meeting the tender of Mr. R. Cosford, to carry out the work, at the cost of £6,322, was accepted by the Committee, and shortly afterwards the work was commenced. The necessary machinery for washing was purchased at the price of £4,859 17s 0d., and a disinfector at the price of £306.

1908

Mr. G. Gardam, the Farm Bailiff, resigned early in 1908 on a Superannuation allowance. Mr. B. Smalley was appointed in his stead.

The question of providing a small isolation Hospital was considered towards the end of the year. This was accordingly erected by Messrs. W. W. Roberts, Limited, at a cost of £2,285 102 0d.

1910

At the meeting of the Committee of Visitors, held at the Asylum on the 15th September, 1910, the following resolution was moved by the Chairman (Mr. W. Hirst Simpson), seconded by Mr. A. Cockerill and carried unanimously:-

"That the Committee of Visitors of the County Asylum at Berry Wood, desire to express their deep sense of the loss that has been sustained by the County in the death of the late Lord Spencer, and their grateful recollection of the important share that he took in the provision and improvement of their great institution, as well as the promotion of all good work for the benefit and good government of the County at large. They are, too, well aware of the severity of the blow which by his death has fallen upon his family, and desire, while expressing their own sorrow, to be allowed to offer most sincere and hearty sympathy with all the members of his family."

Farming and Gardening Account

RECEIPTS	£	s.	d.
Sums received during the year from Sales	635	2	8
Value of Goods supplied to the Asylum during the year			
Beef, Mutton, Pork, etc	48	9	3
Poultry and Eggs	51	2	7
Milk	1007	8	6
Potatoes and other Vegetables	503	13	1
Other Items			
Hay, Oats and Beans supplied to House and Van Horses	45	18	2
	2156	11	7
Carried forward	2791	14	3

EXPENDITURE	£	s.	d.
Value of Stock at the commencement of the year	1857	3	6
SUMS PAID DURING THE YEAR IN RESPECT OF –			
Labour (not that of Patients) 582	6	0	
Provender	348	1	3
Seeds and Manure	74	16	5
Stock, Live (bought)	1178	4	0
Stock Dead (bought)	111	7	2
Harness Repairs	7	5	5
Rates, Taxes, and Insurance	32	17	5
Rent paid	30	0	0
Veterinary Surgeon	10	0	0
Sundries	3	15	6
	2378	13	2
Carried forward	4235	16	8

WORK DONE IN SHOEMAKER'S SHOP DURING THE TWELVE MONTHS

NEW WORK

125 Pairs Men's Boots and Shoe-Made
16 Pairs Men's Slippers Made
83 Pairs Women's Boots and Shoes Made
43 Pairs Women's Slippers Made
51 Pairs Men's Uniform Slippers Made

REPAIRS

{	Pairs Men's Boots and Shoes	Soled and Heeled
630}	Pairs Men's Boots and Shoes	Heeled
{	Pairs Men's Boots and Shoes	Uppers Repaired
{	Pairs Women's Boots and Shoes	Soled and Heeled
829}	Pairs Women's Boots and Shoes	Heeled
{	Pairs Women's Boots and Shoes	Uppers Repaired
{	Pairs Men's Slippers	Soled and Heeled
433}	Pairs Men's Slippers	Heeled
{	Pairs Men's Slippers	Uppers Repaired
{	Pairs Women's Slippers	Soled and Heeled
363}	Pairs Women's Slippers	Heeled
{	Pairs Women's Slippers	Uppers Repaired
59	Pairs Attendant's Uniform Slippers	

MISCELLANEOUS

72 Pairs Braces
77 Bed Sackings, Etc, Etc.

Average Weekly Cost of Maintenance, Medicine, Clothing, and Care of Patients during the Year ending 31st March, 1906.

	s.	d.
Provisions	2	91/2
Farm		117/8
Clothing	0	5
Salaries and Wages	2	65/8
Necessaries (e.g.) Fuel, Light, Washing, etc		101/2
Surgery and Dispensary	07/8	
Wine, Spirits, and Porter	03/8	
Furniture and Bedding		63/4
Miscellaneous		53/4
	8	91/4
Less Moneys received for Articles, Goods and Produce sold (exclusive of those consumed in the Asylum)		53/8
Total Average Weekly Cost per head	8	37/8
	8	6

Weekly Charge for Paupers from County of Northampton
Weekly Charge for other Counties, Boroughs, or Asylums 13s and 14s
Weekly Charge for Private Patients from 10s. to 17s.6d

WORK DONE IN TAILOR'S SHOP DURING THE TWELVE MONTHS

PATIENTS' CLOTHING MADE
9   Tweed Jackets
130   Corduroy and Tweed Trousers
245   Tweed Vest

PATIENTS' CLOTHING REPAIRED
296   Trousers
272   Jackets and Overcoats
72   Vest

ATTENDANT'S CLOTHING MADE
48   Uniform Stripe Twill Jackets
94   Trousers
3   Overcoat

ATTENDANT'S CLOTHING REPAIRED
143   Uniform Trousers
95   Uniform Coats
59   Uniform Vest

MISCELLANEOUS WORK
Repairing Private Patient's Clothing, 7 Mangle Sheets, etc, etc

MACHINING
Billiard Covers, 2; Blinds, 42; Bed Covers, 153; Rug Linings, 39;
Pillows, 296; Beds, 108; Boot and Slipper Tops, 156; etc.

WORK DONE IN UPHOLSTERER'S SHOP DURING THE TWELVE MONTHS

98	New Beds Made		75	New Blinds Made
12	Old Beds Repaired		23	Chairs Re-covered and Repaired
17	Strong Beds Made		10	Seats Re-covered
214	New Pillows Made		6	Tables Re-covered
12	Strong Pillows Made		21	Cushions Made
10	Feather Pillows Made		20	Kneeling Pads Covered
13	New Bolsters Made		54	Pieces of Carpet Bound
56	Waterproof Bed Covers Made		33	Pieces of Carpet Bound
93	Linen Bed Covers Made		12	Sandbags Made
3	Water Beds Repaired		8	Epileptic Cushions Made
93	Bed Sackings Made		12	New Valance Made. .52 Hearth
14	Bed Sackings Repaired		20	Hearth Rugs Repaired
52	Hearth Rugs Lined			

Cleaning and Repairs to Furniture and General Repairs throughout Building

---

SEWING DONE IN FEMALE WARDS FROM APRIL 1ST, 1905 TO MARCH, 1906

343	Chemises		33	Tablecloths
246	Bedgowns		100	Pudding Bags
183	Vests		12	Muslin Ruffles
163	Petticoats		12	Fancy Dresses
592	Sheets		2	Bed Covers
156	Pillow Cases		20	Ticken Bedgowns
150	Pinafores		20	Ticken Chemises
423	Aprons		1020	Bandages
133	Nurse's Aprons		30	Children's Dresses
320	Dresses		120	Nurse's Uniforms
12	Blouses		156	Nurse's Aprons
114	Drawers		60	Ticken Bags
36	Capes		130	Nurse's Caps
702	Hand Towels		105	Shrouds

DIETARY TABLE FOR PRIVATE PATIENTS

1906. And a certain number of Paupers – the latter not to exceed total number of Private Patients.

WEEKLY – 31/2lbs, meat. 7lbs Vegetables. 7lbs Bread. 31/2 pints of Ale. 2ozs Coffee. 1/2lb of Loaf Sugar. 1/2lb Moist Sugar. 7ozs Butter. 1/2lb Cheese. 4 Eggs. 9ozs Bacon. 1/4lb Flour. 14ozs Rice or Sago. 4ozs Sugar for Puddings. 4ozs Currants or Raisins.

PAUPER PATIENTS

WEEKLY – Males. 1st Class: 35ozs Meat. 10ozs Vegetables. 24ozs Suet Pudding. 108ozs Bread. 3 1/2 pints Ale. 14 pints Tea, Coffee, or Cocoa. 9ozs Butter. 8ozs Sugar. 1oz Haricot Beans. 2 pints Milk. Not exceeding 1 1/2lbs Flour. 2ozs sugar and 1oz of Currants for Puddings. 2 pints Soup.

Males, 2nd Class: 30ozs Meat. 70ozs Vegetables. 12ozs Suet Pudding. 108ozs Bread. No Ale. 14pts of Tea, Coffee, or Cocoa. 7ozs Butter. 8ozs Sugar. 1oz Haricot Beans. 2 pints Milk. Not exceeding 1 1/2lbs Flour. 2ozs of Sugar and 1oz of Currants for Puddings. 2 pints Soup.

Females: 26ozs Meat. 68ozs Vegetables. 10ozs Suet Pudding. 94ozs Bread. No Ale. 14pts of Tea, Coffee, Cocoa. 7ozs Butter, 8ozs Sugar. 1oz Haricot Beans. 2 pints Milk. Not exceeding 1 1/2lbs Flour. 2ozs Sugar and 1oz Currants for Puddings. 2 pints Soup.

Male and Female Patients laboriously employed are allowed 3ozs Bread. 1oz Cheese, and 1/2 pint Beer extra daily.

Female Working Patients are also allowed 1/2 pint Tea at 4 p.m. and 1/2oz Butter. Infirmary Diet at discretion of Medical Officers, Christmas Day: Plum Pudding extra. Associated Entertainments: 1/2 pint Ale or Tea with Cake.

ATTENDANTS

WEEKLY – 7 1/2lbs Meat. 7lbs Bread (may be increased to 8lbs) 7lbs Vegetables. 4 ozs of Tea or an equivalent of Coffee or Cocoa. 1lb Sugar. 3 1/2 pints of Milk (may be lessened or increased). 1/2lb Fresh Butter or 3/4lb Salt. 1lb Cheese or Bacon. Flour and Fruit for Puddings. 14 pints of Ale or 1s per week.

NIGHT ATTENDANTS: 1oz Tea extra. 1/2lb Sugar extra. Special Dinners on Christmas Day. Extra Tea or Coffee or 1/2 pint Ale at Associated Entertainments or when on extra duty.

NURSES AND DOMESTICS

WEEKLY – 3 1/2lbs Meat. 7lbs Bread (may be increased to 8lbs). 7lbs Vegetables. 4ozs Tea, or an equivalent of Coffee or Cocoa. 1lb Sugar. Salt. 1lb of Cheese or Bacon. 3 Eggs. 3/4lb Flour. 4ozs Sago, Tapioca, or Corn Flour. 2ozs Rice. 10 1/2 pints of Ale or 9d a week. 2ozs Moist Sugar. Currants, Raisins or Jam, sufficient for Puddings. Special Dinners on Christmas Day. Extra Tea or Coffee, or 1/2 pint Ale at Associated Entertainments, or when on extra duty.

IDIOT CHILDREN

WEEKLY – 80ozs Bread, 6ozs Butter, 1oz Tea. 3 1/2ozs Cocoa. 6 3/4 ozs Meat. 7ozs Oatmeal or an equivalent of Bread. 4ozs Haricot Beans. 6ozs Flour. 11ozs Sugar. 7ozs Rice. 10 pints Milk. 2ozs Currants or Raisins. 56ozs Vegetables.

The above Table for Attendants, Nurses, and Domestics, is drawn up for the convenience of the Storekeeper and Housekeeper, and cannot be demanded by an Attendant, Nurse, or Domestic; nor can any overplus be taken from the Asylum.

4ozs Suet Pudding contains 11ozs Flour and 3ozs of Suet. 1oz of Tea to each gallon. 4ozs Cocoa to each gallon. The Soup consists of 4ozs of Meat and the Liquor from the Meat of the previous day, with Vegetable and Pearl Barley added.

1913

It was the sheer number of patients that became the predominant feature and the Annual Report of 1913 records that "for the first time in the history of the institution the number of inmates reached 1000 on November 15th." This was hardly the most convenient time for such hefty numbers because war was about to make its presence felt, and during the following year 11 members of staff, including a medical officer, left for active service. This was to be resolved, if that is the right word, on July 1st 1915 when a letter was received from the Board of Control stating that more hospital accommodation for sick and wounded soldiers was urgently required in the Midlands. As Northampton occupied a position which fulfilled the requirements of the War Office the Committee of Visitors, with the approval of the County Council, felt it their duty in the time of National Emergency to offer Berry Wood to the Military Authorities. The War Office gratefully accepted, and while the massive task of dispersing the 1105 patients to hospitals elsewhere in the Midlands got underway, discussions began on what alterations were necessary to fit the buildings for their new role.

1915

Northampton Herald
28 Oct. 1915
THE COUNTY ASYLUM
HOW IT BECOMES A WAR HOSPITAL

To the meeting of the Northamptonshire County Council, held at Northampton today, the Committee of Visitors to Berry Wood Asylum presented a special report concerning the use of the Asylum as a hospital for wounded soldiers.

For some months past patients of other asylums now used as war hospitals have been under treatment at Berry Wood, and the Committee pay tribute to the staff for the way in which they cheerfully and willingly discharged the extra duties thrown upon their depleted numbers.

The report continues: "It was indicated by the authorities that another asylum in the midlands was urgently needed. The Committee of Visitors felt it to be their duty and their pleasure to place Berry Wood and their services at the disposal of the War Office, on the conditions that the county suffered no financial loss and that patients were properly provided for to the satisfaction of the Board of Control. "Their readiness to assist has been accepted by the War Office, and arrangements are being made to distribute the present inmates in other institutions within easy reach and to provide accommodation for new cases as they arise. This is not any easy task, but it is being carried out with every desire and effort to cause as little inconvenience as possible to the Boards of Guardians, the patients, and their friends.

"The present staff will be retained for duty in the hospital and will not rank for superannuation.

"The Committee of Visitors feel convinced that the Council will approve of their action in this national emergency."

1919

During the two years, ten months that Berry Wood operated as a War Hospital over 25,000 patients received care within its walls and the "great service rendered to the Country" by this action was proudly placed on record. On March 22nd 1919 the last of the wounded servicemen left and the mentally ill patients began to return from the asylums which had given them temporary shelter.

One would have expected many years of inactivity to elapse while the Institution found its feet again after the War. This, in fact could not be further from the truth because the 1920s saw many developments, and by the 1930s activity – especially in the field of medicine was carried on at a breathless pace. For example, in 1921 there were 19 women patients being nursed under open door conditions and in "home-like surroundings" – a feature which some wanted to see extended to the male side of the hospital in the not too distant future. There was also another simple but important innovation at this time which allowed a number of "trusted patients" to have a late supper and sit up until 9.00 p.m. (long after the normal bed-time) in an area to be known as the Club Ward. And the following year "cinematograph apparatus" was installed for the amusemen

Berrywood Wartime Hospital 1915 –

Photographs –

Recuperating on the lawns on a summer day.

Soldiers able to help in hospital grounds.

Wounded soldiers and first war ambulance outside main entrance.

Berrywood Hospital

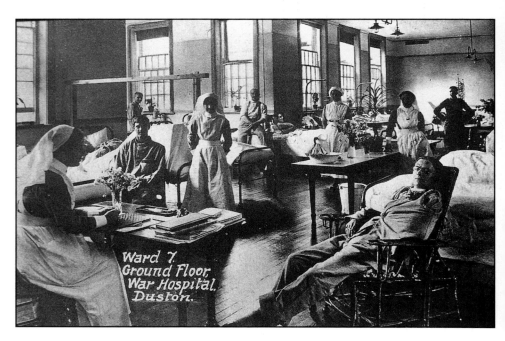

Main dining hall.

Nursing staff awaiting more
war casualties to arrive.

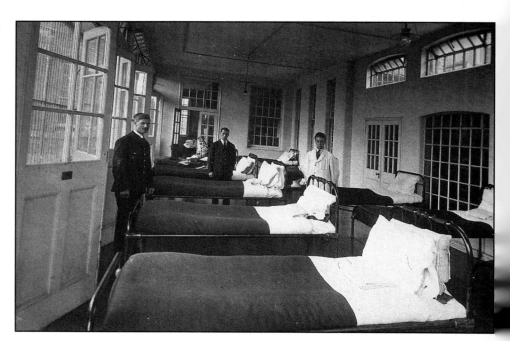

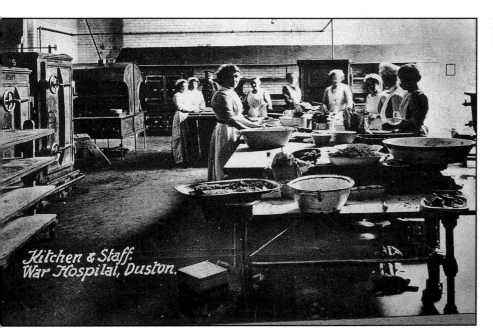

Kitchen and Staff, War Hospital, Berrywood.

Kitchen & Staff.
War Hospital, Duston.

Reception Room.

Main entrance, War Hospital, Berrywood.

Main Entrance, War Hospital, Duston.

General view, War Hospital,
Berrywood.

West wing, War Hospital,
Berrywood.

Ward at War Hospital,
Berrywood.

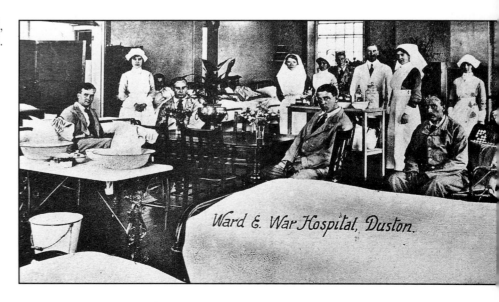

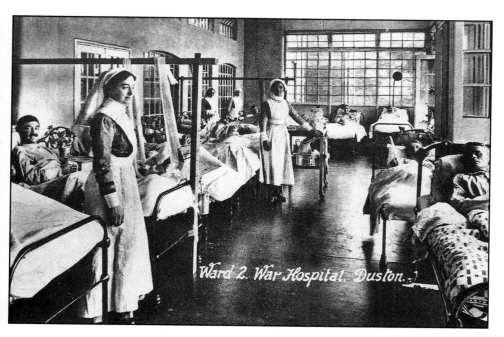

Ward 2, War Hospital, Berrywood.

One of the wards filled with war casualties.

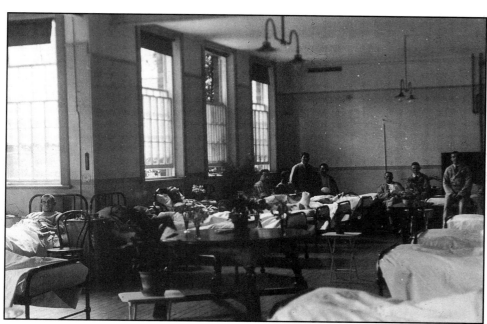

Ward 7, First Floor, War Hospital, Berrywood.

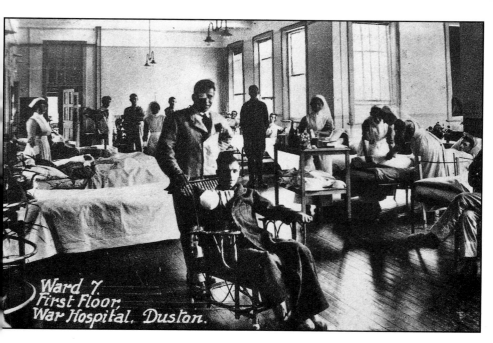

1915

Wartime converted London bus for bringing wounded soldiers from Castle Station to Berrywood Hospital.

of patients. However, it was some 10 years before the talkies arrived, but when they did it was gratefully noted that there was an increased attendance at the film shows.

Other small items which must also have made their own contribution to improving life were the installation of letter boxes in the day rooms, and the use of flowers, plants and pictures to brighten the wards. More importantly, an increasing number of wards were being run on the open door system during the day; while full parole was granted to some 20 men, and another 15 women were allowed limited privilege within the estate. A dentist was appointed to visit the hospital once a fortnight, and by 1926 a major advance appeared with the installation of electricity. This, in turn, enabled X-ray equipment to be installed two years later, and a pathological laboratory was fitted up by 1929 – long overdue, according to the Commissioners.

The perimeter wall and fence around the estate were still maintained at a height of at least six feet, and were regularly patrolled at weekends to ensure that members of the local community did not stray into the grounds. The vast majority of the hospital's doors were still locked, windows were only allowed open three inches top and bottom, and there were single rooms with bars at the doors and shutters where some of the more violent inmates were incarcerated. And, as one might expect, keys were still very much in evidence, and were now considered something of a status symbol – the larger the bunch the more senior the member of staff.

Although nurses were normally working a five-day 60 hour week their life was still rigorous, and their training limited. They began at 6.30 in the morning and were on duty until 7.45 p.m. with three 25-minute breaks for breakfast, dinner and tea. They were duty bound to live in the hospital for the first three years of their service, and until a Nurses Home was opened in 1936 they slept in small single rooms off the main wards and dormitories. Although staff food was generally better than that of the patients, the last meal was served at 5.00 p.m. and there was often a feeling of hunger among the nurses. Some decided to supplement their diet by "pinching" left-overs from the Matron's tray when it had been dispensed with, while at the same time going without food on their off-duty day to ensure that their weekly wage stood at £1. If they were lucky colleagues would obtain some dry bread and a little butter to see them through the day. Sunday tea, however, was a meal not to be missed – it was a "real treat" with two cakes and a banana.

For the patients, meal-times could well be one of the few things that punctuated their day, particularly if the weather was poor. Like that of the staff, their food could be described as possibly sufficient, but certainly very simple – the menu being solely dictated by cost. The hospital's bakehouse produced massive 8lb loaves which were sliced about an inch thick. One of these slices would be served for breakfast together with porridge and perhaps interspersed once or twice a week with sausage or one slice of bacon or an egg. Lunch was normally a meat course, with whatever vegetables were in season from the farm, and a pudding. Patients who were ill or ailing received supplemented diets which included fish and rice pudding. Tea – the last meal of the day – was again based on one slice from the 8lb loaf, probably accompanied by a small portion of jam or fish paste. The small number of patients who were allowed to stay up late were given a mug of cocoa and yes, another slice of bread.

1912

Berrywood Hospital Chapel, built after the main hospital. For a period of time, funerals and internments took place at St. Michael's, Upton.

The eating of meals too, was still governed by strict rules. During the early years spoons were the only implement which patients were allowed to use, and when specially adapted 'safe' knives and forks were introduced there was many an uncertain heart among the staff, perhaps with some justification because despite the fact that every piece of cutlery was counted after each meal a patient still managed to swallow a fork – an action which was only revealed many months later when an X-ray examination was carried out after which the fork was successfully removed.

Like the counting of cutlery, the general furnishings were still very much designed with safety in mind, plus the added necessity of durability. In the day rooms almost everything was simple and heavy and was essentially difficult to use as a weapon against the fellow patients or staff. In the dormitories there were still

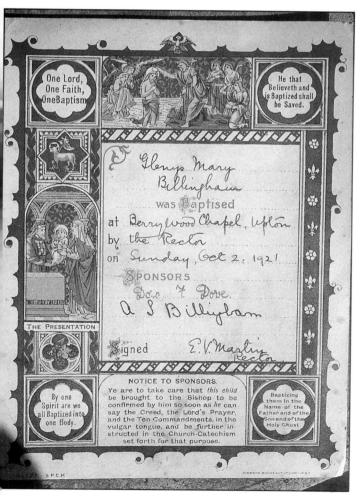

Glenis Billingham's baptismal certificate at Berrywood Chapel.

iron bedsteads – almost certainly provided when the hospital first opened some 60 years before – and the horse-hair mattresses, which were regularly taken to the upholstery shop to be "re-upholstered" and the horse hair washed and teased out afresh.

Assuming the weather was reasonable the practice of turning patients out into the exercise yards for two hours in the morning and another two in the afternoon was still a part of daily life, and, as in previous years there was nothing for them to do but trudge round the walks within the walled courts. For those who were luckier – and capable of carrying on some form of employment – there were still the grounds to be kept in good order, work on the farm, tree-felling, cutting ivy from the hospital's ivy-clad walls or keeping the undergrowth down in the woods. There were also grass cutting machines – towed by two, four or six patients – in use throughout the grounds, and preparation work for the various staff sporting activities, such as marking out the cricket and football pitches or the tennis courts. In fact, it was considered very much a part of the male nurses duty to carry out some of this work himself, even to the extent of one digging the graves, and two more being on hand to lower the coffin. Nursing staff would also be washing bottles in the dispensary and ringing the church bell on Sundays. But supervising one of the work gangs was at least something active to do – for the attendant in charge of those patients trudging round the airing courts it was a task of sheer boredom. One such nurse remembers wishing someone would succeed in jumping from the yard "so I could run after him just for a change."

As with virtually every other aspect of the Hospital's daily routine, the self-supporting skills such as a cobbler, tailor and engineer were also still very much in existence, and the farm was clearly in full swing. There had been constant additions to its buildings and equipment, including a milking machine, and by the mid 1930s the holding consisted of a flourishing market garden and soft fruit orchard from which a high proportion of the produce was used by the hospital. Some say the orchard was also used by the staff after dark!

The large dairy herd provided milk, while sheep and pigs were being maintained for breeding and for fresh meat to be slaughtered at the farm's own slaughter house. All this was complemented by an extensive stock of poultry which ran free-range over many parts of the estate. Incidentally, there was also at this time one solitary peacock – the sole survivor of a considerable number which used to roam through the main grounds. No-one seems to know why they were there, except perhaps they were fashionable during some period and provided the patients with a small interest. But the strange and distinctive calls for which peacocks are renowned must have added weight to any suspicions or misconceptions which were held about Berry Wood by the community outside.

Yet despite so much correspondence with life as it had been when the Asylum was in its earliest days, 1930s was a period when attitudes and legislation changed dramatically, and when at last treatment, as opposed to straightforward care, began to make its impact.

From the very beginning of Asylums anyone who was committed to such institutions knew they were quite likely destined to remain there for life. In such circumstances, with discharges running only a little above nil, the inmates became a static and steadily ageing population. However, the Mental Treatment Act of 1930 paved the way for change – although it was some time before it had any great impact at Berry Wood. Nevertheless, for the first time it actually gave the opportunity for people to seek voluntary admission and treatment, hopefully at an early stage in their illness.

At the time the Commissioners in Lunacy recorded that by 1932 only four patients were resident in the hospital on a voluntary basis, and they hoped that when the provisions of the Act became better known, greater advantage would be taken of it. However, within a year they had hit on a far more likely, and serious, reason for the lack of voluntary admissions – that of overcrowding. This was now becoming a very serious problem in the eyes of the Authorities, with the books constantly showing in excess of 1000 patients, and mattresses having to be laid in the ward corridors at night. The Commissioners considered it quite understandable for voluntary patients to find the overcrowded wards and dormitories "distasteful" and that even if they agreed to be admitted such patients would no doubt discharge themselves earlier than would be the case in more congenial surroundings.

Considerable thought was given to this problem, and it was soon agreed to build an admission hospital and a convalescent villa, both of which had recently been deferred through a lack of finance. By 1935 the Pendered Hospital and the convalescent block were opened it was indeed a development which clearly encouraged the admission of voluntary patients as the Authorities had hoped. The public rarely associated Pendered with the Berry Wood Complex, and accepted it as a separate hospital for those who had nervous break-downs. Apart from this the Pendered was to become a centre for establishing new ideas in treatment. There was now an enthusiasm for the future.

1936

In addition to these considerable steps forward in medical treatment, 1936 was to witness another equally valuable development – that of occupational therapy. Although very much in its earliest form, perhaps making brushes and other simple equipment for use in the hospital and supervised by nurses rather than trained occupational therapists, this work was to develop in later years to become one of the first mental hospital industrial workshops in the country. And, as a more enlightened understanding of the therapeutic which patients could derive from this type of activity continued other similar schemes were begun. Yet again, many of them have been extended to form a valuable part in today's care of the mentally ill. For example, during the same year that occupational therapy began to find its feet, a small group of patients were taken on their first ever holiday. Understandably there were some qualms about how the patients would behave but, as had been proved so often, their conduct was, in many cases markedly improved.

With such developments taking place within the walls of the hospital it is hardly surprising to find that the Authorities were also looking to the greater community outside. Once more, we find the birth of a service which has steadily developed through the years to its role today. It was as early as 1930 that an out-patient clinic, run by the Hospital's Deputy Medical Superintendent, was set up for the treatment of "mental disorders" at Northampton General Hospital. Within a matter of years the Commissioners in Lunacy were commenting upon the success of this operation, and noted that there was also a social worker attached to the clinic. By 1936 two doctors were running the clinic, and a third was holding a weekly child guidance clinic at Dallington Children's Home.

While all these advances were taking place, there were of course a number of improvements to the Hospital itself – a properly equipped operating theatre was provided for the first time; two years earlier in 1935 an automatic telephone system was installed – until then there had only been 12 extensions throughout the building, compared with the 170 or more found today; and the steam fire engine, an old favourite, was finally condemned in the interest of speed and safety, to be replaced by a stationary motor pumping set and chemical fire extinguishers. And, during 1933/34 proposals were adopted to discharge the Hospital's sewage into the Northampton mains. This action was no doubt prompted by a major outbreak of typhoid which killed nearly 30 patients, and affected a great many more. Before the decision to place Berry Wood on the mains system the Hospital had run its own sewage disposal service by allowing the sewage to run over the land. The site had long been noted for its virtue of natural irrigation, and this probably accounts for the excellent crops produced by the farm!

Overcrowding was nearing its peak, with wards of well over 100 patients and just one nurse to care for them at night; infectious diseases such as diphtheria, enteric fever and dysentery were all promoted in these packed conditions; nurse training was limited to weekly lectures of one hour after a 13 hour day on duty, with a written and oral examination at the end of three years which could confidently be passed providing you knew the Nurse Handbook from cover to cover.

All in all, from staff's viewpoint, work at Berry Wood during the early 1930s was low paid, hard, largely repetitive and involved dealing with patients who needed every basic care. As a result staff were not attracted through a feeling of vocation, but on hard economic grounds. At the time of the 1930s recession, felt so bitterly in the North-east where many staff were in fact recruited, the would-be nurses looked upon the work as a secure and pensionable post. Nevertheless they developed a loyalty to the hospital, to each other, and to their patients. Undoubtedly born out of difficulty and hardship it was this attitude which enabled the advances, and the general enthusiasm for the future to develop. Tragically it was to be knocked for six by the Second World War. Unlike the 1914 – 18 War, Berry Wood did not, on this occasion become a Military Hospital. Instead in its already overcrowded state it found itself the recipient of still more patients, this time evacuated by the bus load from other institutions.

With the number of in-patients reaching almost 1400 during and after the war years the effect on the organisation is not difficult to imagine. The few areas available for entertainment such as the recreation hall, were turned into dormitories; there were more mattresses than ever on the floors, and only inches between the beds. Staff shortages were greatly accentuated, thanks to the call-up, and the majority of patients transferred from other hospitals were long stay cases in a very deteriorated state. Add to this the problem of maintaining a black-out with scores of windows which had never seen a curtain over them in the history of the hospital; the difficulty (which caused the Commissioners in Lunacy great concern) of ventilating the dormitories at night; food rationing; and of course air raids. This last problem provided one of the biggest headaches – large numbers of patients had to be shepherded about the hospital to the safest accommodation which could be found, usually in the centre of the complex or partially underground. For example, a newly built general bathroom for men also doubled up as an air-raid shelter for 250 patients. It was hardly surprising then that existence and survival became the sole objectives – as they did throughout the British nation. Unhappily, survival was not to be for two unfortunate inmates. As the Commissioners in Lunacy recorded in their 1943 annual report the majority of the ward gardens had to be closed. "This regrettable state of affairs is due to the fact that in recent weeks a number of patients have been found eating horse chestnuts, a habit which has resulted in two fatalities."

1936

The effect which the War had on the hospital was to leave its mark for many years, and in its way greatly over-shadowed the inception of the National Health Service in 1948. All the enthusiasm which existed during the 1930s was lost and the basic struggle for survival set the hospital back in so many ways – the treatment and care of patients, staff morale and the physical condition of buildings. Things were only just beginning to recover and pick up again by 1948, but there was still a desperate lack of money and initially national resources were almost entirely directed towards general hospitals. As was pointed out by the hospital's first Management Committee set up under the new Health Service the "old evils of outworn buildings, overcrowded wards, and the shortages of staff remained for some years unabated."

However, even if it took a little time to make itself felt, the overall impact of the 1948 National Health Service Act was unquestionable. Management by local government was gone, and although the new Hospital Management Committee was somewhat doubtful about its inheritance, Berry Wood was setting sail in a new direction. This can be best illustrated by two simple facts – the Berry Wood Asylum and the County Mental Hospital (with all the connotations which arise from the words asylum and mental) no longer existed. In their place had been born the St. Crispin Hospital, Duston.

ADMINISTRATIVE AND CLERICAL STAFF (Circa 1943)

POST	SALARY/WAGE		DUTIES
Clerk and Steward	£59. 8. 1d per month		Administratively responsible to the Medical Super
Deputy Clerk and Steward	£34. 8. 1d per month		In charge of all Supplies
1 Cashier	£ 4.12. 8d per week	)	All financial matters including Wages
1 Junior	£ 1. 7. 3d per week	)	All financial matters including Wages
1 Stores Clerk	£ 1. 13. 0d per week	)	
2 Part-time Clerks	1s.3d (6d approx) per hr.	)	Supplies
1 Shorthand-typist	£ 2.15. 7d per week	)	Secretarial (Admin)
1 Part-time Shorthand-typist	1.3d per hour	)	and Statutory Work
1 Shorthand Typist	£ 3.7. 0d per week	)	Secretarial
1 Part-time Clerk	1s. 3d per hour	)	(Medical) and Medical Records

OTHER SALARIES AND WAGES AT SAME PERIOD

Chief Make Nurse	£27.14. 6d per month
Deputy Chief Male Nurse	£22. 9. 7d per month
Matron	£20. 6. 8d per month plus free board and lodging.
Deputy Matron	£16.11. 8d per month plus free board and lodging.
Kitchen Superintendent	£16. 5. 3d per month plus free board and lodging.
Senior Charge Nurse	£ 5. 0. 9d per week of <u>60 Hours</u>
Senior Sister	£ 4. 1. 8d per week of <u>60 Hours</u>

Cost of keeping a patient in the Hospital – £ 2. 2s. 9d.

Berrywood Nursing Staff

Nurses' 1st Year's Examination, March 1909

1. A patient has broken a window and has received a wound in the palm of the hand from which blood is spouting. Remembering how the injury was received, state fully what you would do in such a case.
2. A patient, when out walking in the fields, has slipped and severely sprained her ankle. State what you would do for the injury, and what means you would adopt to bring the patient home.
3. Give the names and positions of the arteries in the upper and lower limbs, and state where compression by the fingers to control bleeding can be applied.
4. A patient who has escaped is found by you lying unconscious three miles from the Asylum. How would you proceed to find out the cause of the unconsciousness? What would you do for the patient? Would you have the patient brought back to the Asylum?
5. There has been an escape of gas in a room on the ground floor and someone is lying unconscious from gas poisoning. Describe what steps you would take to get the patient out of the room, and what you would do for the patient.
6. Why is it of the utmost importance when dressing wounds received in an injury to see that they are perfectly clean?

Mrs. Peggy Billingham

(sister in law to Miss Billingham of Duston)

Mrs. Billingham of Alderton. Her two brothers came from Lincolnshire around 1908 to work as male nurses at Berrywood.

Mr. Billingham then lived in Berrywood Cottage with Mrs. Billingham. The father came from Cople, Beds.

Mr. Billingham married and lived in Duston for 5 years before they were allowed to live as man and wife in cottage accommodation in Berrywood.

Cottages were 3/6 a week, chimney swept, and one or two rooms decorated each year.

Mrs. Gough

Mrs. Gough went to Berrywood as training nurse in 1936 and stayed in the Nurses home soon after it was built. Altogether then some 100 girls were living there on its 3 floors. The nursing examinations were supervised by Mr. Jones, the Duston School Headmaster and the head medical officer of Berrywood. Hours of duty were 6.30 to 7.45, 1/2 day off in 7 days, and an occasional Sunday off.

After passing her examinations to be a Ward sister she recalls being in charge of the Childrens' Ward when some 30 or 40 children were all part of Berrywood until the Princess Marina Hospital was built in 1971. Most of these children needed to be dressed, undressed, washed and hand fed and the caring never ceased night and day. Her ward was considered the hardest of all.

Talking to Mrs. Gough and other nurses, not only did they devotedly care for them but they learnt to love them.

Sometimes a child would die in their care, sometimes with no known parents. Emotion and tears would be shed. Only the nurses with flowers would accompany this forgotten child to the little cemetery at the Church in the Hospital.

In 1940 wards were overcrowded, with patients from the bombed areas added to the Hospital. She later spent a long time with the sick in the Hospital. A & B rooms at Berrywood were for women patients.

Mrs. Margaret Davies

Mrs. Davies was born in one of the Berrywood staff cottages on Berrywood Road. Although she married in 1931 and spent most of her life abroad, she recalls the days as a young girl. Little was seen of her father owing to long dedicated hours at the Hospital every day. She led a devoted life to look after the patients. Her father came from Lincolnshire where she said advertisements for staff in the early days were preferred from this County. The advertisement included that it would be helpful if the applicant could play a musical instrument. She said father played the violin and so helped make up the entertainment in the large hall. She also speaks of the full Chapel at Berrywood where all male patients sat on one side and female the other and her mother would sit with her in the Gallery. Both her parents are buried in Upton Church. During the first War she recalls seeing the fire at the Bishop's Bakehouse (now the bottom shop opposite village school). All the village turned out as the thatch blazed. Also a group of soldiers from war time Berrywood came. Eventually the fire was put out but the property was altered and that was the end of the Bakehouse. Some of the remains of the ovens still remain in the very thick walls.

(Late) Mr. Beadle, Charge Nurse

Mr. Beadle began work at Berrywood in 1921. He talked about long hours of duty as a male nurse. The duty was from 6.30 a.m. to 7.45 p.m. with half an hour for dinner and 25 minutes for tea. There was an alternate spell of duty for night attendants. He was responsible for over a hundred patients in his ward plus a nurse. Part of his duty was to take a group of male patients to the farm fields to get vegetables for the kitchens. Each man was allocated a tobacco issue. In each male ward was a gas jet by the fire for lighting their pipes, as was in the kitchen garden, and one gas jet in the Head Gardeners potting shed.

I asked him about straightjackets for uncontrollable cases in the main block but he replied "no". They wore padded clothes and were in a padded room. Some of the bad cases they had to feed, but not very often was this necessary.

He used to take a large group of patients to Berrywood Chapel. At one time he spoke of it being packed in the old days, and had a fine Choir of Men and Women Nurses.

Mrs. Rachel Rowell

Mrs. R. Rowell began training as a nurse at Berrywood in 1935. She then went to Pendered ground floor and her duties varied from working in the kitchens and general duties on the ground floor reserved for staff and day nurses.

Later as a trained nurse, she worked in the Childrens' Ward and in the Old Isolation Hospital wards.

She remembers women in padded clothing, then for their own protection. Jack, her husband was also a qualified male nurse. Both came to work at Berrywood but were not allowed to live together there for five years after they married and could not fraternize.

Mr. Jack Thompson

Mr. Jack Thompson and his sister were brought up at Berrywood, their parents being both nurses at the Hospital. To get married, their father had to get living accommodation outside the hospital, so they went to live in Beechwood Road, both continuing to work at Berrywood.

Mr. Thompson recalls how all the key workmen, Laundry, Engineer, Baker lived in cottages within easy call of the Hospital. His father drove the first Ford van for the Hospital, collecting essential food supplies etc.

All the suppliers delivered their produce to a central depot at St John Station from where he collected it. The various firms were not allowed into the hospital.

The continual coal supply was an exception and these horse-drawn wagons were allowed in, 2 wagons at a time, as 2 horses were needed to pull each wagon up Old Duston Hill.

Mrs. Scott

(Aged 95) 20 years Ward Nurse

Sometimes she had 113 Patients in her care. Women Patients who had certain mental illness affected by the phases of the moon and nurses had to be prepared for sudden outbreaks of uncontrollable behaviour.

She remembers that the violence of some of the patients could be so strong at peak times of recurring mental violence. She remembers glass smashed, iron bedsteads torn apart, and the metal bent and thrown about.

At the centenary celebrations in 1976, she recalls a large cake with 100 candles on it. There she met nurses again, also previous staff Matrons met Senior Nurses.

Mr. William Burrell

(Retired) Secretary and Finance Officer

In 1962 Mr. Burrell came to Berrywood and so began at St. Crispin and a time of great change inspired by him after many years of Oxford Regional Management, slowly began the change of attacking Mental health as an illness and excluding the stigma, so much so that ultimately the whole structure of the Hospital was to improve. High entrance gates were removed, high walls were taken down to remove the prison-like sombre appearance and a five year plan to redecorate all wards etc. So more freedom for the patients was allowed and eventually a time of enlightment and pride began to emerge by all culminating in a better health average for the patients.

1969. Industrial Therapy unit was established on the Berrywood Rd, where old and new skills were encouraged and extra money could be earnt, thanks to Northampton Chamber of Commerce and the help of British Timken.

Eventually this County Hospital was so transformed that it became the envy of Countrywide Mental Hospitals. Mr. Burrell was later to travel in advisory capacity to many other institutions up and down the country.

Mrs. Munday

(Domestic)

Mrs. Munday was responsible for the domestic duties in three senior doctors' houses in the hospital in the years 1930 to 1936, and occasionally was called upon to help in the main kitchens that prepared the food for all the women. Patients would be peeling large quantities of potatoes, cutting up cabbage and cauliflower etc, peeling apples, baskets at a time, placing them in large copper containers for Hospital ovens. After this large amount of food was cooked, it was collected by staff and trollied to the various departments and placed on a large area of hot plates, a fixture in all the wards to be able to serve the food warm. She remembers the childrens' ward being near the cinder track (west black walk) where the mentally handicapped and physically handicapped children were looked after until adult age when they went into the main wards. This all changed when Princess Marina Hospital was built.

She recalls all the permanent skilled men who had workshops there; butchers, carpenter, baker, painters and decorators, boot and shoe repairers, electricians etc, mostly Duston men that found employment there.

Mr. Arthur Clements Harpole

(Aged 90)

Mr. Clements was at Berrywood for 36 years. By 1921 he was Deputy in charge of Refectory Ward, 1925 Dept. Chief Male Nurse, 1935 Chief Male Nurse. His wage in 1943 was £27. 14s. 6d per month. His hours 50 years ago were often only £2 a week. Night duties were on a rota system. During the last war he was in charge of 100 patients until the morning in the overcrowded hospital. Included in his normal duties was to help wash, shave, and dress some of the patients. Due to transfer of patients from other parts of the country in 1940-45, he said beds were everywhere and his charge rose to 650 men patients.

He relates an interesting story regarding the manual fire pumps at the farm which needed 3 men either side to operate, drawn by a horse. One day a fire alarm was sounded (but the fire was put out quickly by hand). The Chief Medical Officer afterwards enquired why the manual pump did not arrive. "Well Sir", the farmworker replied, "the horse had gone to market! It's Wednesday." Mr. Clements recalls the night bomber during the last war that dropped a string of incendiaries that fell either side of Berrywood buildings and a child later carried an unexploded bomb into one of the houses. Patients that were well enough went on a holiday to Redcar during the summer. In the winter, a film show operated and was staffed by male nurses every other week. The event of the year was at Christmas, an annual fancy dress ball for patients and nurses. All this helped to create a family friendship. When a patient was fit again mentally to face the outside world, tears would be shed by the nurses and patients, recalls Mr. Clements.

1878 – 1890

Female nurse in uniform of the early years
of the hospital.

This area of water in front of the main entrance and offices, was said to have been there as a standby for water supply in case of a serious fire in the early years of the hospital.

The old laundry about 1900.

1891

Nice view of the hospital.

The old boiler house, built 1875
(now demolished).

1911

Lady (unknown) walking in the well kept walks of
the hospital.

1910

Staff cricket team included
Mr. James, Harry English and
Dr. Stuart.

1915

Staff at Berrywood Hospital
included Mr. James, Dr. Stuart,
Miss Irons and Mrs. Sharp.

1910

Demonstration of new fire
fighting equipment to nurses
and general staff on the lawns
outside the hospital.

Nurse photographed in front of the heavy iron gates, at the main entrance (Berrywood Road) sometime before the first war.

1912

Ready for stage play.
Mr. James, and Dr. Stuart. The Matron on the right,
Miss Stewart and lady unknown.

The old staff cottages on the Berrywood Road.

1918

Male nurses, all smart in their striped uniforms.

1918

The 1914 – 1918 Wartime Hospital.

Convalescent Home, Berry Wood

Nurses in costume for their annual ball.

Nursing staff were welcomed years ago, that
could play a musical instrument, to occasionally
play at hospital concerts.

1887

Mrs. Smalley with village school children proudly wearing their jubilee
medal on 27 June 1887 in the grounds of the hospital.

1908

Miss Ann Jones dressed for the annual Christmas ball at the hospital.

1906

Ann Jane Jones, nurse in uniform.

1913

Berrywood windmill destroyed by gale.
(Pump house still stands)

1911

John Faulkner, Duston village postman outside Mr.
Bailey's farm cottage.

Part 6 – Berrywood Farm

George Gardam came to newly built Berrywood in 1875 and built up the first herd of dairy cattle sheep and poultry etc. He also managed the kitchen gardens, recruiting staff to supply the food for the entire Hospital patients which were to number some 1400. His daughter Mary married William Spokes from Upton Mill. Both are remembered by older parishioners. William held high office in the affairs of the county and Mary for her long years in office as President of Duston W.I. from 1926-1955, one of the most respected members of the W.I. In retirement they lived in Millway. William's great grandson John still farms at the Mill today.

Mary's other sister Lucy married a Mr. Fox and lived in one of the two brick houses that stood in Mr. Major's park land (Highfield) now included in Saxon Rise. George Gardam's son Dacre, a teacher by profession, on his retirement from London, built Church View in Church Way, where Mrs. Faulkner Gammage now lives. Her late husband enlarged it. William, the eldest son of George, later Headmaster at Rushden, first went to live in Peveril Road and raised a daughter, Christine, and twin sons, Clifford and Bert, whom the writer had the pleasure of meeting in Duston Churchyard some 15 years ago, looking for the family graves. Both had emigrated to Australia and were approaching retirement. Bert today is with his business empire in Brisbane aged 85, a millionaire. His brother Clifford, on his early return to England became headmaster at a school in Chelmsford. He died a few years ago and his daughter Tanis and her husband together with their great friend Mary Smeathers, provided me with the Gardam's history.

Billy Gardam's wedding (to his second wife) at St. Luke's Church. His twin boys emigrated to Australia (Cliff and Bert).

On horseback in early days in Australia. Cliff and ranch hand with brother Bert Gardam standing.

Wedding group. Lucy Gardam to Mr. Fox. Lucy was sister to Mary Gardam who married Mr. William Spokes of Upton. She is remembered for her wonderful work as president of Duston W.I.

1875

Mr. Gardam, first manager of Berrywood Farm in his pony and trap outside All Saints Church.

Mr. Gardam photographed about 1880.

Farm workers then would either thatch corn hayricks or cottages.

1935

Mr. Billingham with working horses.

Mr. Billingham (centre of photo) with working patients have a break from the harvesting.

1889

Present from Miss Gardam (school teacher, Duston) to William Billingham.

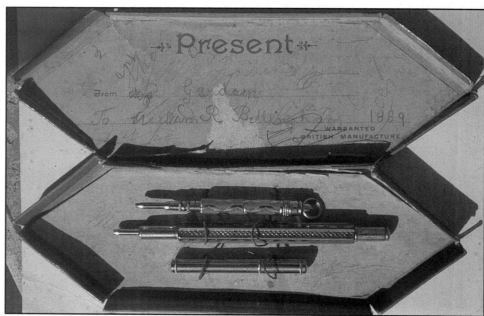

18th century farm workers' personal beer barrel and horn breaker used by William Billingham.

1932

Megan Billingham outside farm cottage.

Medal to commemorate Queen Victoria's Jubilee 1887. Given to Robert William Billingham at the village school. It was a day's holiday.

1932

Mr. Ward with Megan Billingham on his shoulder.

1907

Farm cottages where the Bailey
Family then lived.

1912

Photographed in the head
medical officer's car.
William Bailey, Harry Eason
and Fred Bailey.

1909

In their Sunday best.
Fred, Harry, Baden,
Kathleen and Mary Bailey.

The Bailey Family, Fred Bailey, Mary Bailey, Albert York (Bailey), Kathleen Bailey and Barden Bailey.

Fred Bailey at his father's cottage at Millway.

Kathleen Bailey as a young girl. She died in 1993 aged 93. The last of the family who once lived at their Berrywood farm cottage.

1908

After Sunday service at Berrywood Chapel.
Kathleen and Baden Bailey.

1935

Kathleen and Miss Douz.

Harry Bailey with his father's bees.

1916

Harry and William Bailey emigrated to Canada. This is the wooden house they lived in, the Wheatlands of Ontario.

The four horse team at plough in Canada.

1948

Fred Bailey feeding his poultry at Roade. Retired, he, like his father, was a well known beekeeper.

1936

Steam engine belted up to saw bench ready for work.

Sawing timber for use on the Berrywood estate
(fencing posts etc.)

1910

Fred Eason, waggoner, moving heavy timber at farm (boys in their best suits looking on).

1910

Henry Downie, friend of the Bailey boys in his football jersey, photographed at the farm.

1910

Potato harvesting in the old fields, now part of Marina Hospital.

Harvest scene at Berrywood Farm.

1923

Henry, Tom and John Billingham at Berrywood Farm.

1906

Sheep shearing at the farm.

1880

The first steam engine used for stationary work around the farm buildings.

1975

Showing the old steam engine shed and the old piggery in front of the main farm entrance.

SLOW
PATIENTS
CROSSING

The old footpath from Upton to Berrywood across the fields.

1908

Mr. Smalley and family in his own manager's garden.

1908

Children in wooden tub on the pond, once in front of the farm entrance.